30 SECOND SUCCESS

Laura Templeton

HIGHLANDER
PRESS

Published by: Highlander Press
Editor: Deborah Kevin
Cover Design: Hanne Brøter
Interior Design: Catherine Williams, Chapter One Book Production, UK
Author Photo: Brenda Jankowski
ISBN: 9781734376401

"This enjoyable book provides you with strategies and insights to understand how to do networking the right way. And when you do it right, you will achieve wonderful results. Period. Laura's engaging and direct style makes this book a true page-turner!"

Mari Carmen Pizarro, High-Performance Executive Coach, Speaker, Author and Founder of International Women's Leadership Academy

"Panic. Every person who has ever had to introduce themselves at a networking event, or explain who they are and what they do, has experienced it. Laura Templeton's new book 30 Second Success takes the fear out of delivering our "elevator pitch," as well as more extensive public speaking, by asking us to determine our "why" and concentrate on building relationships. Her practical tips and well-thought-out, strategic approach make this a book everyone who speaks in public (meaning EVERYONE!) should read!"

Mary Fran Bontempo, 2x TEDx Speaker, Author—*The 15 Minute Master*

"If only someone had written this sooner... Being the Founder of a relationship company, I would recommend this to any of our Members. Teaching the key fundamentals on how to build rapport, tell your story, and making new connections is vital for success."

Robert Wilson, CEO, and Founder of OnDoc

"For entrepreneurs, sales executives, and professionals responsible for business development, networking is essential to growing relationships that lead to revenue. However, one of the biggest mistakes these business leaders make is investing time, energy and resources into "networking" and getting little to no results. That is where Laura Templeton comes in. Laura has mastered the art of building relationships and converting them into referral partners and clients. In her book, she shares her most practical networking strategies to "ditch the pitch" and start building meaningful connections to grow your business."

Brynne Tillman, The LinkedIn Whisperer, and CEO of Social Sales Link

"Laura has created a tried and true method to get clear, concise, and comfortable with your messaging while still staying true to yourself. In this book, she provides a roadmap that explores your why and will help you thrive, building both professional and personal connections. Laura recognizes the value of networking as a business strategy. She has seen that value firsthand for her own success and her book will help many others realize that the first 30 seconds can be the beginning of real magic."

Jennifer Lynn Robinson, Esquire CEO Purposeful Networking

"I'm a networker. I network quite a bit. I thought I had my thirty-second pitch down; that was until I met Laura, and she helped me perfect it. Laura is someone you need in your corner for optimal success in business networking, and her book is an extension of this. Easy and approachable, this book is a guide to making a lasting impact in just 30 seconds with everyone you meet. I highly recommend picking it up and reading it until the binding falls apart. Great job Laura!"

Seth Goldstein, Principal Creative Director – Goldstein Media and Founding Member of Startup Bucks

"Anyone can benefit from Laura Templeton's new book *30 Second Success* regardless of experience. I have a lifetime of speaking, sales, and networking experience, and yet I found 3 areas where *30 Second Success* can help me with my new endeavors. Those 3 areas are: finding my "Why," looking for a niche, and keeping my networking introduction refreshed. Laura knows what networking is about and shares it in *30 Second Success* when she says, "Networking is not about selling, it's about RELATIONSHIPS." *30 Second Success* will be my go-to business book gift for years to come."

Margye Solomon, Diverse Small Business Advocate and Chief of Staff at Envision2bWell

"Laura creates a framework for effectively and concisely communicating your message. She teaches you a formula and method of thinking, which leads you down a path that helps you find your voice. Never struggle again with what to say when given the opportunity to introduce yourself to a room of potential clients and referral partners."

Brenda Jankowski, Award-Winning Lifestyle Photographer at BrenPhotography

"I have spent the last 30 years perfecting my networking skills. The first thirty-second impression often decides the direction of the relationship so spending time perfecting that part of your professional game is wisdom. Tools like LinkedIn are invaluable for identifying those you should be networking with but there is no substitute for face to face interaction. Laura's networking experience shared within these pages is a game-changer for a young professional or anyone who wants to move their business to the next level."

Rick Millham, Jr., CIC, President, Millham Insurance Agency

"Laura Templeton is at it again! Only this time, we don't have to take notes rapidly because her powerful wisdom is in print! If you think you're strong in networking, read this book! If you're terrified of public speaking, read this book! Expert and novice alike will gain valuable nuggets to apply in helping them grow and achieve more than they can imagine."

Jacquline Condict, Executive Leadership Coach, Conduit Connections, LLC

"The fear of public speaking, or glossophobia, is dreaded by so many, even to the point of diminishing one's ability to effectively communicate a simple elevator pitch of 30 seconds. If you are one of these people, fear not, as Laura Templeton has developed the perfect toolkit for those who struggle at networking events. Laura suggests you start with your "why" to focus on the "who" you are serving. Having witnessed Laura's expertise first-hand on more than one occasion, I can assure you that she has mastered her craft and provides excellent guidance to help you deliver a winning introduction to build relationships at networking events, instead of sounding "salesy." To be in the first violin seat, or be a star athlete, or deliver a polished pitch, it will take practice, but you need to have a successful framework. You will certainly find that in this *30 Second Success* book."

Lynne M. Williams, BS, MA, ABD, Executive Director,
Philadelphia Area Great Careers Group

"Laura Templeton is a master networker. She has been networking for many years and has helped hundreds of people find their thirty-second message. She has combined her expertise and experience into this powerful book, *30 Second Success*. Check it out and learn how to connect with your message and grow your network."

Chip Baker, Creator of Chip Baker – The Success Chronicles

"Knowing "why" you are doing what you are doing is so instrumental to your success, and Laura gives us a clear picture of that. If you know your "why," then you can figure out your "who" you want to serve. Always keep your why in front of you at all times! It will get you through the hard times. Laura is clear on her why and how she helps entrepreneurs to their thirty-second success! And she nailed it when she said that networking is about relationship building. Knowing your thirty-second success will help create more networking and relationship opportunities! Keep up the great work Laura!"

Jo Hausman, Go For It! Media Group, Speaker & Best-Selling Author
Go For It! A Woman's Guide to Perseverance

For the love of my life, my kids, my g-babies and my God.
Thank you for believing in me.

For my network and my readers.
May you never again struggle to find the words that
express your true message.

Table of Contents

Introduction

The room quiets, and all eyes are on me, it's my turn. What do I say? Oh no, I forgot my script, and I can't read my scribbled notes. How am I ever going to get through this? My palms sweat, my heart races, and I feel like I have cotton in my mouth...wait, I can do this...for goodness sake, SAY SOMETHING!

Okay, calm down, you can do this. You know these people, you've done this a million times before, but you always get nervous, why is this so hard? Okay, here goes...

Uh, hi. I'm Mary Smith. I'm a photographer. Uh, I do family portraits, newborn babies, weddings, life events, uh, headshots, oh, and product photos. My studio is located at 4112 Sunny Lane, two miles down the road from here. Uh, I can take pictures inside or outside. My prices are very reasonable. Uh, you can buy a package of images or pick the ones you want, a la carte. When you're ready to schedule your session, call me. Thank you.

Well, that wasn't so bad. Oh shoot, I forgot to tell them about my Mother's Day special this month. Oh well, I can tell them at the end of the meeting. Wow, I can't believe I even forgot to bring my flyers. Uugh, why do I come here? This is such a waste of time!

Does this internal monologue sound familiar? If you were to change the product in the statement beginning with "I sell…" to insurance, real estate, web development, banking services, coaching, or whatever you sell, can you hear the monologue unfolding?

Maybe this sounds like you, or maybe it's someone you've networked with. The point is, everyone knows someone who struggles with what to say when faced with the opportunity to give their thirty-second message to a room full of potential clients and referral partners. Let me tell you a little secret: it doesn't have to be that hard. REALLY!

Networking is a great way to expand your connections and your business when done well, but most people struggle to effectively communicate who they are in thirty seconds or less. This ultimately equates to lost opportunities.

Trust me when I say you can learn to love your network, and you might even learn to enjoy giving your thirty-second message. Well, maybe some of you won't learn to enjoy it, but at least you'll learn to deliver it with clarity and confidence without feeling like you want to run from the room, or worse, stay home.

With more than fifteen years of sales and marketing experience, I've received tremendous high-level sales training and professional development. I've also spent a lot of time working on personal development and have had the privilege of training others in the direct sales field.

I've consistently used networking as one of my main business marketing strategies because word of mouth is still the best form of marketing, and there's no better place to connect and build referral relationships than networking events.

After years of networking, I stepped into a leadership role with a networking organization. As a leader, you tend to look at your members through a different lens. You try to find out what they need and how you can best serve them. One topic continued to bubble to the surface: members needed help with their thirty-second message.

It broke my heart to see people I have grown to know and care for struggle month after month when it was time to go around the room and give their thirty-second message (or as some might call it...your commercial or pitch). I actually had one member who used to leave the room when it was time for commercials and not return until we were finished. Her fear of public speaking kept her from connecting with her audience for over a year.

Glossophobia, which is the super cool and geeky name for fear of public speaking, is very real. In fact, in the 2018 Chapman University study of America's Top Fears[1], more than 25% of Americans reported public speaking as their number one fear. That means that one out of every four Americans has a fear of public speaking. Think about that the next time you are at a networking event. It truly is a struggle for many people.

> *One out of every four Americans has a fear of public speaking.*

I love writing. I love helping people. And I love public speaking. I know—it's okay if that seems odd to you, but I do! I get totally jazzed when I get to share knowledge from the stage that helps someone overcome a problem or struggle. I learned how to craft an authentic thirty-second message that connects with my audience years ago, so naturally, I started offering my services. Then word got out about how I was helping others and requests for me to speak to other groups and organizations started pouring in.

Launching 30 Second Success® in 2015 provided the platform to connect with audiences worldwide. Now I enjoy working with individual clients, organizations, and associations who understand the value of crafting a clear, concise brand message that connects with their ideal clients and the people who know them.

How to Use This Book

Before we dive into the learning portion of this book, I want to take a moment to suggest how to use it. Think of this as your guide to not only crafting your message but to change how you connect with the people you come in contact with every day.

There are two distinct sections to this book. Part One, defining your message, is all about understanding what goes into creating an authentic, heartfelt message that connects with your audience. Part Two details how to make connections with your audience and your network in a way that builds relationships and your business.

If you're like me, you want to grab a pen and some highlighters. There are a lot of great nuggets of information woven throughout this book for you to hold onto. Highlight them so you can find them later on. You'll be amazed at how often you reference them whenever it's time to up your game or change your message.

Grab a journal or notebook to write in. You'll want to have a place to keep your writings as we move through the chapters because you'll be creating your message as you progress through the book. I'll also be encouraging you to write some other insights down that you'll want to reference later on and in the future.

Throughout this book, you'll see this symbol: ✐ This denotes a good stopping point to take time to write your thoughts and ideas down. (Yes, I know it is a left-handed pencil... I'm a lefty and proud of it.)

Keep a copy for yourself. This is one of those books you'll want to re-read from time to time. You'll reference it for the great information and all the valuable nuggets you'll pick up along the way. You may be tempted to give it away or lend it out. Give them their own copy.

Me? I love giving books away to people in my network. Over the years, I started adding the following note to the inside of the front cover:

I liked this book so much, I felt the need to share it. If you enjoy it as much as I did, the only request I have is that you pass it along. If you find yourself in possession of this book and don't have anyone to pass it along to, kindly return it to" (Insert your name and address here) But, be sure to add your name and state inside the front cover, so everyone can see how far this wonderful book has traveled.

I haven't gotten any books back yet, but it will be fun to see how far they've traveled if and when they eventually do come back.

Part One

Part One

It Starts with "Why"

You might be asking right about now, "What does my 'why' have to do with my thirty-second message?" and I really don't blame you. But stick with me here, and you'll understand soon enough that your "why" has a lot to do with your message. In fact, there are a lot of Business Coaches out there encouraging people to share your why as your message. Although I do not wholly agree with that philosophy, I do know that to understand your clients and stay focused on your business goals, you need to understand your reason for doing what you do, hence starting with your why.

Knowing your "why" is very important, especially in business, and it often gives us a better understanding of "who" we serve. This will be especially important as we move forward. When we have a deep understanding of why we do what we do, we often find that it is easier to connect with who we serve.

Often times, it is the connection to a personal need that drives us to success and even though your personal "why" may not have anything to do with who you serve, why you serve that particular client, the story behind what you do and why you believe in it, will certainly matter. Whatever your why, it is important to know and to keep in view as you grow your business,

> *Knowing your "why" gives you the fuel that feeds your confidence to stand fast and deliver an excellent thirty-second message.*

especially on those days that challenge you and make you question your sanity for sticking with it.

If I told you, *"I help people create their thirty-second messages because I want to take a trip around the world."* that might sound shallow and a bit selfish to most people (maybe not a travel agent) because there's a disconnect that is hard to overcome. But, if I told you, *"I help people create their thirty-second messages because I've seen too many incredible people I have come to know and love struggle to deliver a clear, concise message month after month,"* that would most likely get you to sit up and listen if this is something you struggle with because it is authentic and elicits an emotional connection.

So why do you do what you do? Do you want to:

- ✦ Create a legacy for your family;
- ✦ Change the lives of people in a third world country;
- ✦ Successfully impact 1 million entrepreneurs worldwide;
- ✦ Start and fully fund a non-profit to fund research for a cure;
- ✦ Help people escape poverty by providing them with an opportunity to build their own success story; or
- ✦ Never let another person struggle with their thirty-second message (Oh wait, that's mine).

In the 2009 TED Talk, *How Great Leaders Inspire Action*[2], which has been viewed more than 44 million times as of the date of this writing, Simon Sinek explains that "people don't buy what you do, they buy why you do it."

In his talk, using Apple as his example, he discusses how companies that focus on their why in their messaging have record-shattering sales and inspire loyal followers. While record-shattering sales may not be true for all, solid sales and loyal customers are typical for those who keep their focus on their why.

"Apple is dedicated to the empowerment of man—to making personal computing accessible to each and every individual so as to help change the way we think, work, learn, and communicate." That was Apple's original mission statement, according to marketing guru and Interbrand Pacific founder David Andrew.[3]

Now, your "why" or mission statement may be far simpler than that; the point is, it needs to be specific. It needs to connect on a deep emotional level with you and your clients. That's how you create a loyal following, with your core values, your "why", your mission in mind.

As a business owner, professional, or an organization, it's crucial to know what your company "why" is and to keep it as your primary focus for all of your messaging. What is the impact you want your business to have on the world? Whatever your "why", write it down, keep it in sight, know what it is for those days when you face challenges that stretch and strengthen you. Not only will it keep your messaging on point, but it will also keep you motivated and focused, especially when things get stressful. Identify your "why" now, if you have not already done so.

✐ Write your "Why."

Take some time to define and really express your "why" if you have not already done so. Post your "why" where you will see it as a daily reminder. Consider the following questions as you write:

- ✧ **Why do you get up every morning and get to work?** What about your business inspires you to face each day and gets you going even when you would rather not?

- ✧ **What are you passionate about?** What resonates with you deep in your soul? Is it helping people, a charity, volunteering, what? What or who drives you and keeps you focused on your "why"?

✧ **Why will people be drawn to you?** People are drawn to individuals and companies that have a direction. Your "why" helps you create and focus on your goals. What are your goals, and how are they connected to your "why"?

Revisit your "why" periodically, it may change from time to time. Just like goals, once we achieve them, we then get to decide what we will focus on as our next goal, on our next "why".

Why Network?

When I first started networking as a direct sales consultant, I had no clue what I was doing, I was just looking for a way to connect with business owners in need of my products and new people to talk to. What I found was a network of women who would give me so much more.

I found a group of women who wanted to hear what I had to say, and not just about my products, they actually wanted to get to know me, the business owner, the corporate refugee turned stay-at-home mompreneur. They wanted to help by telling their friends about me and offering to help however they could. Even if they didn't need my products, they knew people who did and were happy to connect us. I had found my network.

Many people show up at networking events to gather as many business cards as they can, tell anyone who will listen all about what they do, schedule appointments to tell them more, and then go in for the sale. I bet you know several people that fit this description. I bet you also steer clear of people who fit this description too.

Most people who network know that networking is a really great marketing strategy for business. There are plenty of opportunities to meet people who fit your ideal client avatar and plenty of people who know your ideal clients and may be willing to make introductions. But, how do you get them to do that without being "salesy"? *Relationships*.

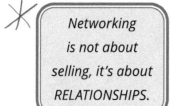

Networking is not about selling, it's about RELATIONSHIPS.

Networking is about building relationships. It's about developing the **know**, **like,** and **trust** factors with the people you connect with. Have you ever heard the saying, "People do business with people they know, like and trust"? The best approach to networking is to build a foundation of trust among the people by forging relationships with them.

There will be different levels of relationships within your network. You will spend more time with some people than with others, have more in common with some, and be more comfortable with others. The point is, by letting go of the selling mentality and focusing on building relationships, you will get to your ultimate goal.

Yes, the ultimate goal is about increasing your business, there's no denying that. But that is not what you should be focusing on with networking. The bigger picture is that building relationships is the key to long-term business. It's about nurturing connections that will serve you well into the future with referrals and repeat business.

If you don't have time to invest or if you don't like people, don't tackle networking! You'll only get frustrated. Let someone else in your company do it for you. You could even hire someone to network on your behalf.

Pick someone with a great personality who enjoys meeting people. If they ask you a lot of questions and want to grow your relationship and understand what you do, chances are good, they'll be a great networker for you.

The real point here is that building relationships takes time. If you're willing to invest the time, the rewards are well worth it!

Overcome the Fear

What's keeping you from networking? Is it meeting new people? Is it not knowing anyone at a meeting or event you've been invited to? Is it having to start conversations and introducing yourself? Is it not knowing what to say or knowing that you'll have to tell everyone what you do in your thirty-second message when all eyes are on you?

These are all valid fears, but guess what... you're not alone. Everyone in the room started out exactly where you are now. Everyone at one time or another was a newbie. In fact, you might not even be the only new person at the meeting when you do decide to go.

> *Everyone in the room was new to networking at some point.*

Stop letting fear hold you back! Here are some tips to help you overcome your fear:

- ✧ **Overcome the fear of making a mistake.** No one but you will know if you mess up. Trust me, people are not that observant. They won't remember from week to week or month to month if you mess up. What they will remember is that you made an effort and will applaud you for it. If they don't, find a new group.

- ✧ **Overcome the fear of not knowing anyone and going it alone.** All you need is one friendly smile to get you past this fear. Every networking group has a leader who will welcome you and help you acclimate to the group. They are vested in your success. After all, they want you to come back. Ask them to introduce you to the two most interesting people in the group and get to know those folks.

✧ **Overcome the fear of not knowing what to say.** Learn to be a good listener. Ask a lot of questions and get to know the people in the room. You'll feel more comfortable and confident as you get to know the group, and you'll warm up as you answer their questions. You might not always know what to say or know the right thing (if there is such a thing) to say, but if you speak truthfully and openly, you'll do just fine.

✧ **Overcome the fear of public speaking.** Remember glossophobia mentioned in the introduction? It's a real thing, and one out of every four people in your networking group struggle with it. Isn't that comforting? You are not alone. There are several techniques to help you overcome this fear, and the most important one is being prepared. Know your business like no one else. What do you want people to know about you and how you serve your clients?

This is why you bought this book...to help you craft an authentic message that will help you connect with your audience and get them to want to know more. But it is more than just creating the message. It's about how you deliver it with confidence and clarity that will connect with your audience on a deeper emotional level that inspires them to want to know you.

Confidence and clarity come from belief. Belief in your product or service, belief in your company, belief in yourself and your ability to deliver what you say you will. I am always amazed at the transformation that takes place for

> *Confidence and clarity come with belief.*

my individual clients when I present them with their thirty-second messages for the first time.

My ability to extract what my clients do and add an emotional component to their thirty-second message seems to give them the direction they are looking for. It's as if they have permission to tell the world how awesome they are because I see it in them, I believe in them.

Another technique that helps overcome these fears is to practice. Practice what you will say. Practice shaking hands and smiling. Practice with a friend, family member, or in a mirror. One of my favorite places to practice my message or a speech I am preparing to deliver is in the car. For years I used to keep a written copy of my thirty-second message in my car. I'd read it at red lights until I had it memorized, then I'd keep on practicing. The benefit of all that practice is that it kept me focused on the message and not on the emotions, causing my stomach to somersault. After all these years, I still practice on my way to meetings.

> *Fear is natural for everyone. It's what you choose to do with that fear that matters.*

In a 2017 article[4] published by the Mayo Clinic, Craig N. Sawchuk, Ph.D., L.P. answers the questions, "How can I overcome my fear of public speaking?"

Dr. Sawchuk answers the reader by sharing that the "fear of public speaking is a common form of anxiety." He also says that "Many people with this fear avoid public speaking situations altogether, or they suffer through them with shaking hands and a quavering voice."

Does that sound familiar? Here's my take on some steps that may help you overcome or at least manage this very common fear.

✧ **Know your topic**. No one knows your business like you do. Be the expert you were meant to be. If this is a new business, share that. Your network will understand if you are still learning everything. They will be rooting for you as you grow. Trust yourself; you've got this!

✦ **Get organized**. Knowing what you want to share and knowing who you will share it with can greatly reduce your anxiety about speaking. Find out as much as you can about your audience ahead of time, this will help you prepare for what you want to share.

✦ **Practice, and then practice some more**. By now, I hope you know how I feel about practice! If not, I'm sure I'll be sharing my thoughts on the matter again in the coming chapters. I will say though, practice doesn't take a whole lot of time. You could practice in the car on the way to a meeting. You'll also get more practice the more you network. Think of every opportunity to share your message as an opportunity to practice.

✦ **Challenge specific worries**. Sometimes we make things out to be worse than they are in our minds. Challenge those thoughts and put them in their place. What's the worst thing that could happen? What's the probability that it would happen to you? What's the probability that if it happened to you, it has already happened to someone else, and they will be there to help you through it? That's how people who network support one another. Even if the worst were to happen, there would be someone there to help you through it. My suggestion: learn to laugh when the unexpected happens. People laugh with you, and it doesn't seem all that bad after all.

✦ **Visualize your success**. Visualization is a great tool to help you experience the desired outcome you seek. Knowing who you want to connect with and how you will connect with them is part of that. It's like role play for your mind. Just be sure to focus on the positive outcome and keep your mind from wandering.

✧ **Do some deep breathing**. Deep breathing is a great technique. Be sure to focus on slowing your breathing and the sense of calm that you want to create with it. Don't forget to breathe out! Many people hold their breath without realizing it. When you focus on your breathing, focus on breathing in and out slowly.

✧ **Focus on your material, not on your audience**. When you know your topic, you are much more prepared to speak about it. Remember, in a networking environment, everyone has been in your shoes at one time or another. They are rooting for you to succeed.

✧ **Don't fear a moment of silence**. If you lose your place or forget what you wanted to say, take a moment to collect your thoughts and continue. No one knows what you are going to say, so even if you jump ahead, it's all good. A pause can give your audience a moment to ponder what you've said. It gives them time to process what you've said and to lean in to hear more. It truly can be a good thing, even when unintentional.

✧ **Recognize your success**. Accept the applause. Be careful not to criticize yourself for a missed word or statement. There is always room for improvement when you consider every presentation as practice for the next opportunity.

✧ **Get support**. Seeking help is why you are reading this book. Congratulations on taking a positive step to improve your message and your presentation skills. You can do this!

I'd encourage you to **trust your audience**. Networking is like connecting with a big support group, it's about trusting the people you surround yourself with to support, understand, and promote you. They are vested in your success, so naturally, they will cheer you on as you become more confident in your message and your presentation skills. With the right message and plenty of practice, you will be able to overcome your fear and effectively deliver your thirty-second message whenever the opportunity arises.

Find Your Niche

Have you heard the phrase, "The riches are in niches?" There's a lot of truth in that when it comes to marketing your business.

If you only work with small to medium businesses with up to $50 Million in revenue, market to them. There's no sense in marketing to the entrepreneur or billion-dollar companies if they aren't your niche. One of my clients is a business growth specialist. He helps small to medium businesses in the $500,000 to $10 million-dollar range evaluate their companies and find expansion opportunities. He knows his sweet spot.

Drill down to what you really want. Who do you want to work with? Yes, give yourself permission to work with the people you want to work with. Be specific about who they are. What do you focus on specifically that can make the most impact? What sets you apart?

If you're a realtor who works with veterans, you may have the occasional civilian contact you, and you can work with them if you want, but the focus of your message should be on veterans.

I recently connected with a virtual administrator who only works with business coaches. He really knows his niche and offers specific services that coaches need. Another

> *Drill down to what you really want.*

virtual administrator in my network works specifically with realtors. She understands their market, their forms, their timetables, and their marketing styles. Same business, with totally different clients.

✐ **Take some time to really think about your niche**. Do you have one? Do you want one? Why not create one for yourself. When you get really specific and focus on what you want to do and who you want to work with, you start to find those people just about everywhere you look. Even more importantly, they begin to find you because your message is tailored specifically to their needs.

Have you created a niche for yourself? I have. By identifying that I help business owners, professionals, and sales teams with their thirty-second message for networking, I have created a clear focus on my ideal client. I can help with business development, branding, marketing, content, and so much more, but to be super specific about thirty-second messages sets me apart in my industry and my network as an expert in this very specific niche.

A word of caution for new business owners, when you first begin developing your business, what you offer your ideal client may continue to fluctuate. Over time, you continuously refine your services and offerings to fit the needs of the people who come to you. As you grow your business, a niche may begin to emerge for you. Allow yourself time to experience who you work with, who gravitates to you, and who you gravitate to. If you find that there is one particular type of client that you enjoy working with, start to tailor your services and your message to that particular client.

One of my clients, a health and fitness coach, found that she loved to work with new moms looking to regain their "before baby body." She knew this would be a challenge given that there are many fitness studios in her area offering similar classes. What she found out after a little research was that most new moms want to bring their babies along, but don't want to put them in childcare. She developed a class that allows moms to actually workout with their little ones. Classes fill up in no time now, and other studios send moms her way.

When you find your niche, and you begin to tailor your services and message to them, more will find you. It is a given that you will begin to attract the people you want to work with. That's not to say there won't be others, it's just that if your calendar is filled with the clients you really enjoy working with, you'll be able to choose if you want to work with the ones that don't fit, or not. Life is definitely more enjoyable when you get to choose.

> *When you know your niche, more of your ideal clients will find you.*

Your Ideal Client

When working with new clients, I often find that they are lost in the weeds for who they serve, who they love working with, and who needs their services. This is the primary reason they can't figure out their message.

> *Your ideal client is the person or people you provide a product or service to; the people who need your product or service.*

When it comes to identifying your ideal client, all too often, either you don't have a clear picture of who they are, the picture has changed, or the description is too broad, and the picture is blurry. This is one of the areas I really love to explore with individual coaching clients. Now it's time to identify your ideal clients and where to find them.

How do you serve your clients?
Yes, serve! This is the key to making great connections with people. This question is a great starting point to

> *We are called to have a heart of service.*

help gain a better understanding of who your ideal client is. How you serve your clients may be unique to you even if you work in a very competitive market. How you serve your clients often sets you apart from your competition.

One of my real estate clients prides herself on creating a positive experience for first time home buyers by educating them on what to expect, even the unexpected, while another focuses on bringing quality connections to clients that help them prepare their homes as they downsize. What do you do that attracts clients to you?

Digging deep into this question will help you convey your unique message to the clients you wish to attract.

As you know, to understand others, we must first understand ourselves, or at least we must first understand our business.

Here are **five key elements** to explore in order to better understand who your clients are.

✐ **Take time to answer the following questions. Your notes will be very helpful now and in the future.**

1. Know who you are.

Amazon and eBay seem to have something for everyone. They serve a multitude of clients and businesses at multiple levels, but that may not be practical for your business. Answer these questions for yourself:

✧ **What do you like to do?** (as related to business as well as personally) Sometimes what we do in our free time connects with what we do in business. For instance, I know a personal trainer who loves to golf, he has developed a fitness program specifically for golfers to help them improve their performance and increase their stamina.

✧ **What makes you unique?** Think of your differentiators. Your experience, or perhaps lack of experience, can often work in your favor. It's all in how you position it. What I mean here is that as someone with years of experience you know what your clients need and how to deliver it quickly and concisely, and as someone new to the industry you bring a fresh perspective along with the latest innovations that allow you to give your clients what they need quickly and concisely. See what I mean?

- **If you have competition, what sets you apart?** Why would someone work with you instead of the guy down the street? How you treat your clients, what value you provide, and the end results they can expect all contribute to what sets you apart. And believe me, it doesn't always come down to price, good customer service will get you more clients and referrals than you could ever dream of.

  If you aren't sure, ask your network, ask the people closest to you or some of your favorite clients for their thoughts. You might be surprised. Someone recently asked me what my unique proposition was, I had a good idea, but I decided to ask my mastermind group for their thoughts about it. Their answers really helped me gain better insight into how I serve my clients on a deeper level than I actually realized. If you're unsure how to answer this, reach out to your closest business connections, those people who know you, know your services, and understand how you serve your clients.

- **Has your business changed over time?** Will it continue to change? Evaluating your business and how you meet client needs is critical to your success. Business changes, especially how you connect with clients and how you market products and services. Are you willing to change with your business? If finding new clients means changing how you do business, would you? You need to be prepared for change, or you might get left behind.

  My business is very different today from when I started.

There are services I've dropped because they drained me and the services I've added because my clients needed them, and I enjoy developing them with the help of my clients. Being willing to change and grow is all part of the life of your business.

2. Your favorite clients.

✧ **Who do you like working with?** Think about some of your favorite clients. Reflect on who they are, what they do, how you help them, and why you enjoy working with them so much. I know one Content Writer who enjoys blogging for Lawyers and another who blogs for Veterinarians. Yes, they write for other clients as well, but all of their marketing and messaging is directed at their favorite people to work for in the market they are most knowledgeable.

✧ **What did you like about them?** Was it their attitude? Were they open to your ideas? Did they pay on time? What one thing or combination of things made you a little sad when you finished working together?

✧ **How would you describe them?** Describe their personality, their presence, how they made you feel when you worked together. Think about their appearance and how they conducted themselves. Were they reliable, did they show up on time?

✧ **Are they willing to work for their success?** There's no point in working with someone who isn't willing to work. Their success is often a reflection on you, making wise decisions on who to work with and who to avoid can often be traced to this question. They need to be willing to implement the work you do together.

- ✧ **Where did you meet them?** Go there! Know where you've met some of your favorite clients and make a point to stay connected to the same network, the same people, or the same type of network and people. Chances are where there's one there's more, and they talk to one another.

- ✧ **If given the opportunity, would you work with them again?** That should be a resounding, "HECK, YES!" Why not work to find more clients just like them?

3. Know your competitors.

> *Don't think you don't have any competition... you're fooling yourself if you really think that.*

Don't think you don't have any competition, I thought that. Then I did a little search on the internet and found several people with similar business offerings. Granted, no one focused on my specific niche of helping people uncover their thirty-second message that resonates with their audience, but there are some folks out there focusing on creating your pitch.

- ✧ **What do they do?** Know your competition and what they offer. Don't worry if you offer the same thing, just know that you do. It's all good! Clients will be attracted to you for a different reason. Be the best version of yourself and trust that there is plenty of business to go around.

- ✧ **How do they stand out?** What makes your competition unique? You might find that they focus on a particular demographic different from your own. Here's a great opportunity for you to attract your demographic and refer theirs to them.

✧ **What qualities do you admire about them?** This is really important because it will help you view them in a positive light. When you talk positively about your competitors, people are always surprised because they don't expect it. Be positive and encouraging and learn to work together for the benefit of everyone, especially clients.

There's absolutely nothing wrong with keeping an eye on the competition. Be ethical in all of your dealings and be willing to give credit where credit is due.

I know two social media experts who network together. Their clients are similar but not the same, so they have found a way to support one another without being competitive. They actually help elevate one another every chance they get. Their attitude is that there is plenty of business to go around and they want their clients and connections to get the best care possible.

4. Ask your peers.

Ask the people in your industry and your business associates for their understanding of who would benefit from your product or service. Ask your network, the people you trust, "Who do you think my ideal client is?" A lot can be learned by asking people what they think.

I know a portrait photographer who was struggling for clients. His work is exceptional, but his field is very competitive. In one of my workshops, we were discussing ideal clients when another attendee who is familiar with his work spoke up and shared the experience he creates for families with special needs children and how he makes them feel. He lit up! He has since changed his message, and people are seeking him out because of this new focus based on feedback from someone in his network.

Trust the people in your network to give you feedback on your message. Simply ask them what they think you do for clients. The answer might surprise you, be prepared for truth because you asked for it.

5. Do your homework.

Know your business! No one knows your business like you. Learn all the ins and outs. Be the expert in your field, and if you aren't, find someone who is and ask them to mentor you.

✧ **So, who is the typical client for your product or service?** I often joke that my ideal client is anyone who has to answer the question, "So, what do you do?" but in reality, it's people who network for business and event coordinators hiring speakers to educate audiences on effective communications and networking.

✧ **What's your demographic?** Are you living in an area that supports the physical and financial description of your ideal client? If so, great! If not, you'll need to learn how to become effective at finding and connecting with your ideal clients through your online networking organizations (directories are a perfect place to connect) and through social media.

✧ **What does your customer avatar look like? PAINT A PICTURE!** I have a client who is a financial advisor. She describes her ideal client as a recently widowed mother with a policy her spouse left behind, along with all the bills, the house, and the responsibilities. She's worried about her financial stability, her future, and providing for her children's college education. How's that for an avatar? She even named her Karen!

Here are some additional questions to help you create your avatar. These are just a starting point. I am certain you may think of others that are more specific to your business.

a. What do they look like? This is more about self-care than actual "physical looks" (unless you are a dentist, in which case, you want to know if they have a nice smile or hide their teeth.)

b. Are they male or female? Do you work with men/women/both? Does it matter? For obvious reasons, your business may focus on one sexual preference based on your niche.

c. Are they fit or flabby? This, again, is about self-care. A lot can be learned about a client by their appearance, just ask a fitness expert.

d. What age range do they fit into? Older, younger, adult, child, adult child, Millennial with college debt, Boomer with aging parents, and Millennial living at home with college debt and no job.

e. Do they live near or far? How far are they willing to travel? Are they familiar with Zoom?

f. What type of work do they do?

g. Are they single or married? Divorced or widowed?

h. Do they have kids, and how old are they? Does that matter?

i. Where do they hang out? Likes and dislikes, travel or homebody, etc.

j. What kind of personality do they have? Anxious, depressed, negative (if you cure those things—great!), happy, encouraging, positive, friendly. These are the peeps you want to hang with.

These are just some suggestions. You can go even deeper when you think about your product or service and who it helps the most. Think about your answers regarding your favorite clients and begin to really hone in on the details of your client avatar.

✐ **Got the Picture?** Write it down and keep it close to remind you of who it is you want to work with, who you want to attract to your business, who you serve.

Congratulations, you've got your client avatar! Once you know who they are, it's easier to figure out where they are.

I have a good friend who is an amazing portrait photographer (yes, she's my photographer). She offers the ultimate experience for her clients with a package she created. She knows exactly who her ideal client is, why they would buy her package, how much they are willing to spend, and what they want to feel like during their session. She has created marketing materials and a client intake form that draws you into the experience from the moment you visit her website. She knows that for her clients, the value is in the experience she creates for them at the start. She also knows that her clients can be found within a certain radius, and that is where she networks.

When you're that specific about who you work with, it's amazing how much more in tune you are with where to find them. As you focus your business and your message on the people you want to work with, you begin to attract more of them to you. Yes, you will attract others as well, especially when they hear how wonderful you are from your ideal clients. The fun begins when you get to choose if you want to work with them or not.

Remember to visit your client avatar periodically and update as often as necessary. Business changes often, and sometimes ideal clients change, too.

Powerful Words

The words you choose can make an impact on the listener. The study of how words affect a response in the brain is simply fascinating. Some words, even when spoken in a calming tone, can elicit an angry or pensive response, while other words can be very soothing when spoken in an abrupt tone. It's how our brains are wired to receive these words that make for a unique opportunity when writing a speech or preparing marketing materials.

Do your own internet search of positive, powerful, convincing, and commanding words and phrases, and you'll find numerous lists that make an impact on the listener. These types of words and phrases cause people to react or respond as desired by the speaker. But why? Why do these words and phrases have such an impact on the mind and how humans respond to them?

Why? Because our brains are wired to respond to prompts. For those of us who remember the eighties when computers first came into our homes, there was something called a "command prompt." Are you familiar with that term? Simply stated, you give a command to the computer, and it performs a programmed response. Well, our brains are wired to do the same. We've been programmed to listen for direction. Yes, we have the choice to react, but chances are we will respond positively if it benefits us.

There's a great article from *The Persuasion Evolution*[5], with a list that has grown to over 400 words that have been sorted by the emotional state you wish to inspire in your potential customer.

In this article, Bushra Azhar expresses how words are more than just strings of text strung together. Words are cues, they are triggers that elicit an emotional response. They can take a sentence from one that is dull and boring to one that is vibrant and exciting.

Words can be used to persuade people to act in the manner you wish them to just by the ones you choose. Think about it like the flip of a switch, words can be used to take you through a litany of emotions.

Azhar states in her article that high emotional words "are capable of transforming an absolute no into almost yes and a "perhaps" into "for sure!" Because it isn't really about your desired action, but the underlying emotion that drives that action."

> *"If you get them to feel that emotion, you GOT 'em."*
> —Bushar Azhar

Identify what emotion it is you want your audience to feel when you are sharing your thirty-second message. How do you want them to feel? What emotion do you want them to tap into?

I heard about an insurance agent who loved to share client stories to help her network understand how she was able to help clients reach a fair settlement with the right coverage. The only problem was that she was so good at telling devastatingly emotional stories that half the room would be in tears by the time she was done. Perhaps the words she chose were too strong, who wants to leave a meeting feeling sad, but they were effective in getting her point across.

As you craft your thirty-second message, play with the words you use. Think of how your audience will respond to what you share with them. If you want them to feel empathy toward the person in your story, choose words that elicit that emotion. Know what you want your audience to "feel" when you are creating your message. This will help you choose appropriate words for the reaction or connection you desire for your audience.

Your message is truly about connecting with your audience in a deep emotional way. Understanding the emotion, the feeling you want people to experience is a big part of connecting. When you deliver your message with deep heartfelt emotion, you can't help but evoke emotion and create a connection with your audience.

Thirty-Second Message

When it comes to building your business and your brand, nothing is more important than your thirty-second message. Let's face it, you can spend thousands of dollars creating the perfect logo, website, and business cards, but if your thirty-second message doesn't inspire people to want to schedule an appointment, visit your website, or take your business card and call you later (*really* call you later not just say they will) none of that will matter. Your thirty-second message is your commercial for your business. It needs to be ready to go anytime, anywhere anyone asks, "So, what do you do?"

> *Your thirty-second message is your commercial for your business. It's your pitch, without being pitchy.*

Logic dictates that people really want to know who you are, but the truth is, in this day and age, they want to know how you can help them solve their problem or meet a need that they or someone they know might have. In the sales and marketing world, there's a term for that: **W**hat's **I**n **I**t **F**or **T**hem (WIIFT). What can you do for them that they can't do for themselves? That's what they really want to know.

Conversion is key; just ask the companies that purchase those million-dollar ads during the Super Bowl. They hope that their commercials are memorable enough for people to buy their products based on a deep-rooted desire, a need, or a want. People are hired

> *Conversion is key.*

and fired over the success of such marketing campaigns, but let's face it, not many business owners today can afford to buy big advertising and *hope* that it will work.

Having a truly effective thirty-second message will make all the difference when it comes to marketing and branding your business. People will identify you with your brand because of what you say, how you say it, and how you make them feel.

✎ **Here's where the fun begins.** Time to craft your message, so get your pens ready. (Note: you might want to use a pencil WITH an eraser. Edits are encouraged. The more you let your creativity flow, the more fun you will have with this process.)

What's the purpose of your thirty-second message? Most people think the purpose of a thirty-second message is to educate your audience about what you do by giving them as much information as possible as quickly as possible. They try to fit everything they do into a few short sentences or wind up running on and on about what they do. It's never fun to hear that thirty-second buzzer when you have so much more to say.

The purpose of your thirty-second message is not to educate people on *everything* you do, on the contrary, it is to pique their interest and inspire them to want to know more. The idea is to grab their attention, speak to their heart (remember the emotional state you want to evoke), and inspire them to schedule that first appointment with you to find out more about your product or service.

When you truly accept and understand the power you can harness in just a few short sentences, you will be able to effectively communicate with your audience in networking meetings, business socials and events, one-on-one conversations, marketing material, and social posts, and in front of the camera. In fact, becoming comfortable with the simple, proven formula presented in this book will give you the confidence to effectively communicate who you are and what you do in a variety of situations that you will most likely begin to seek out.

The true purpose of your thirty-second message is to create curiosity and inspire your audience to make that first appointment. It's at that first appointment that you can get to know them, discover what they need help with, and WOW them with the amazing way you do.

> *Create curiosity!*
> *Get them to want to*
> *know more!*

The Formula

There are four key components to every great thirty-second message. As you will see, there are five listed here, but one is optional, and I will explain the reason why I included it and why I say it's optional when we get to it.

According to an article published by *Time Magazine* in 2015[6], quoting a study from Microsoft Corporation, people now generally lose concentration after eight seconds. It stands to reason that it takes most people less than eight seconds from the time you begin speaking to decide if they are going to listen to what you have to say. This is why it is so important to utilize the time you have to grab their attention and create curiosity from the very beginning.

> *It takes less than eight seconds from the time you begin speaking for someone to decide if they want to listen.*

After years of networking and researching how to develop a thirty-second message that captures the attention of your audience and inspires them to want to know more, I discovered a simple formula that works. This is a formula that has been used by leading networking experts and sales professionals for years with proven results.

Here are the key components of the thirty-second message formula:

1. Pain Point
2. Solution
3. A Call to Action
4. A Good Referral (Optional)
5. Who You Are

Let's explore each of these so you have a better understanding of how they work, their important roles in creating your thirty-second message, and how they work together to move your audience to take action. Once you have a clear understanding of this simple formula, you'll be able to create a thirty-second message that connects with your audience in a way that drives more business to your door and makes your networking experience much more satisfying. In fact, many of my clients print the formula on a 3x5 card and carry it with them to help them stay on point when presenting their thirty-second message.

1. Pain Point

What is Your Ideal Client's Pain Point?

First, let's define what a pain point is exactly. A pain point is a problem or issue that your ideal client can relate to.

Begin with the pain. Yes, when you begin by identifying a pain or problem that your ideal client struggles with, you grab the attention of your audience almost immediately. By telling them what pain or problem you solve, they immediately start thinking of who they know that might be struggling with that specific pain or problem.

When you position your message well, you begin to help your audience think beyond themselves to the people in their network. By sharing the problem you solve for clients at the very beginning, you give their minds time to go to work searching their memory for someone with that problem, because, let's face

> *Position your message well to help your audience think beyond themselves.*

41

it, we all want to fix the people we care about. Even if we aren't the ones with the problem, we probably know someone who is.

What is a problem that your ideal client struggles with that you can help them overcome? You might find several problems that you can help your clients address. This gives you options for changing your message periodically, for now, start with one or perhaps the most common one that you address in your business.

Example:

Most people struggle to effectively communicate who they are and what they do in thirty seconds or less.

(This and all following examples for The Formula are taken from *30 Second Success*® message development.)

✎ **Write down your ideal client's pain points on your notepad. Brainstorm everything that comes to mind.** Remember to connect with the "emotional state" you identified earlier. Connecting with their pain is more about the emotional turmoil, how they feel, than about the actual problem itself. If people feel icky about something, remind them how that icky-ness feels with your message.

Presenting the Pain Point as a Question or a Statement

A pain point can be presented in two ways: in the form of a question or as a statement. Presenting the pain point as a question inspires interaction with your audience as does a statement when presented in a way that causes agreement. Again, it's about grabbing your audience's attention from the moment you begin to speak.

When asking a question, raise your hand, and your audience will raise their hands along with you. When you present it as a statement, shake your head, yes, and people will shake their heads in agreement. Getting your audience to engage with you by showing their agreement is a great way to grab their attention.

Even more important than getting that engagement is that you have now successfully identified your potential clients in the room. Think about it…everyone who raises their hand or shakes their heads with you is a potential client or knows someone who is.

Question Example:

Does anyone here ever feel like running from the room or throwing up when it's your turn to give your thirty-second message? **(Raise hand)**

Statement Example:

Many people are gripped with stomach-wrenching fear when it's their turn to deliver a thirty-second message. **(Shake head)**

✐ **Rewrite your pain points as questions or statements.**

Tell a Story People Can Relate To

Another great way to communicate who you are is by telling a story. The story can be yours or one of your clients' stories. People relate well to the story of personal or professional experience. It's much easier to recall a story than it is to recall a name. Stories are a great way to connect with your audience, and to be memorable, stories make it easier for people to refer you.

Be sure to keep the story short and sweet to stay within thirty seconds. If people want to know more, great! That's what your first appointment is for.

Example:

I had a client who would consistently leave the room when it was time for thirty-second messages because she was so overcome with fear. Imagine how many opportunities she missed in her first year of networking.

✐ **Write a quick story identifying a pain point your ideal client will be able to relate to.**

2. Solution

How Do You Solve Your Client's Problem?

Now that you've identified your ideal client's pain point, it's time to position yourself or your company as the solution. I'm not saying you're a miracle worker (unless you really are), but you have something that can help ease their pain, so why not tell them what that is or how you intend to help them. Tell them that you and only you can fix the problem you have just identified for them, a problem they may not have even known they had until this very moment.

> *People want to know you can fix their problem.*

Think about it, in this day and age of instant gratification, what do people want you to do when you tell them they have a problem? They want you to fix it for them. They don't want to go around knowing that they have a problem they can't solve or knowing they have a problem that needs solving, and they need to find someone that can help them. They want to know that you, the person who just told them they have a problem, also has a solution that can fix it for them...right NOW!

What Sets You Apart From Your Competition?

One of the most important things to remember when offering a solution is why someone would want to do business with you. What sets you apart from your competition? These are important questions to consider when offering your solution to potential clients.

Many of us have businesses that are common, or we have the same services others in our network may offer, so offering a unique solution to someone's pain in a way that really connects with their emotions is key.

Speak to their hearts. When we get past the head and speak to the heart, we are connecting on a completely different level. People want to know more about how you can help them personally, what it would feel like to work with you. A strong, specific solution is a compelling reason for people to want to work with you.

Example:

I help people craft a thirty-second message that resonates with their audience and drives business to their door.

Often your solution will begin with "I help." This is an easy way to brainstorm the solution you provide. Just be careful not to overuse "I help".

Example:

At 30 Second Success, we provide business owners and professionals with a branded thirty-second message that resonates with their audience and drives business to their door.

When Telling a Story, Tell What You Did to Solve the Problem

Stories are memorable! It's also a great way to keep the interest of your audience that you see frequently. When you condition your audience to expect a story, they start listening for them, they also begin sharing them with their connections. That's what you want!

Example:

(Remember my client who would leave the room?)
When working together, I was able to provide her with a clear, concise message she now delivers with confidence and a smile!

✐ **Write the solution that you offer your clients.**

3. Call-to-Action

Tell Your Audience What You Want Them to Do

A call-to-action (CTA) is often referred to as "the close." Whatever you call it, you must have it. People need to be told what to do, now that you have told them they have a problem and that you can fix it for them.

Yes, I said, "People need to be TOLD what to do!"

Seriously! You want them to take action, right? Well, telling them the best way to connect with you quickly, will cause them to take action sooner rather than later or not at all. Let's face it, in this day and age, the minute people leave a meeting or event, they forget all about you unless you've made a great impression and even then they may only remember you when they check their email or answer a phone call.

> *Tell them what to do with a strong call-to-action.*

There are certain words in the English language that prompt people to respond. Keywords are like "command prompts" to the minds of your audience. You give it a command, and the desired action happens (or at least it is most likely to happen). By telling someone what they need to do to connect with you, you are, in essence, providing a command to their brain to take action.

For this reason, I am going to ask you to refrain from using the word "please" in your call to action. Some time ago, I heard about a study that was done that focused on response rates for cold calling (making unsolicited calls to people you don't know and have not been introduced too.)

When people made cold calls and left a scripted message explaining the purpose of their call and ended their message with "Please call me back at..." the return rate was 30%. When they made the same calls with the same script and ended their message with "Call me back at..." the return rate was 70%. The only word they left out was the word "please," and their return rate increased significantly.

Tell your mother, it's my fault, but we are tossing out the word "please" here. The reason for the overwhelming increase in the rate of response is that there are certain words and phrases in the English language that act as commands, "please" is not one of them. Our brains are wired the same way. "Please" is wishy-washy and almost says "if you want to" without saying it, while "Call me back" becomes very commanding without it.

What Works for You—Phone, Email, Text, Website, or See Me?

Be very specific in your CTA. What do you want your listeners to do, how do you want them to connect with you, and when? Tell them what works for you: phone, email, text, website, or see me. Short, sweet, and to the point. Again, this is designed to create curiosity and get them to want to know more.

Three CTA Examples:

- ✧ Schedule an appointment today.
- ✧ Visit my website today.
- ✧ Sign up today.

My favorite is "Schedule an appointment today." Why wait? You want them to approach you after the meeting so you can schedule a one-on-one meeting.

Combine Your CTA with a Tagline or a Company Statement

You can combine your CTA with a tagline or a company statement. I love "If" statements leading to your CTA. These are not necessary, but they are a great way to reiterate how you solve their problem. This is a great way to solidify what you do in the minds of your audience.

Example Tagline Added to CTA:

"Ditch the Pitch & Start Connecting!"™ Schedule an appointment today.

Example Statement:

If you're ready to connect with your words in thirty seconds or less, schedule an appointment today.

✐ **Write your call to action.**

4. A Good Referral (Optional)

Who Would Be a Good Referral for You?

There are referral network groups who ask that you identify a good referral as part of your message. Personally, I feel that this isn't necessary for your thirty-second message. My reason for this has to do with your pain point. You've already identified your ideal client when describing their pain points. Your audience has already decided if it's them or someone they know.

Describe Your Ideal Client, Someone in Need of Your Services

> *Bring it back to their pain point.*

If you network in a group that asks you to include this in your message, or if you like including this as part of your message, my suggestion is to bring it back to your pain point. Be careful not to make your "good referral" statement too narrow, thereby excluding some of the people who originally identified with the pain point you've described.

Example:

A good referral for me is someone who struggles with their thirty-second message.

✐ **Write your good referral statement.**

5. Who You Are

ALWAYS End with Your Name and Company

You can begin your thirty-second message with your name and company, but I don't recommend it, especially if you are in an industry with a large representation. You will actually see people in the audience glaze over as soon as you say your company name. Realtors, financial advisors, bankers, and the like really get what I am saying here. Remember, you have less than eight seconds to grab the attention of your audience, and if you start with your name and company, you use up precious time—time better spent connecting with their pain and how you are their solution.

If you have a business or a reputation that will grab attention, then certainly say it first, but make sure to have plenty of time for your pain, solution, call to action, and your name and company at the end. **Keeping your name and company at the end has more purpose than you realize.** You can include your name elsewhere in your message (I will give you some examples further along), and you can also include your title in the end if you like, but you must ALWAYS end with your name and company.

Once you've got their attention and have created curiosity, they are going to want to know who you are so they can write your name down as someone they need to connect with after the meeting. Don't make them ask the guy next to you who you are!

> *Ending with your name and company is a must!*

Example:

Laura Templeton with 30 Second Success.

Example with your title:

Laura Templeton, CEO of 30 Second Success.

✏ **Write who you are.**

Put It All Together

Now it's the time to put each piece of the formula together to form your thirty-second message. You will see in the following examples that the pain point is listed first, followed by the solution, then the CTA, and ending with who you are.

Statement Example:

> *Many people are gripped with stomach-wrenching fear when it's their turn to deliver a thirty-second message. (Shake head)* I help people craft a thirty-second message that resonates with their audience and drives business to their door. *If you're ready to make an impact with your words in thirty seconds or less, schedule a call with me today.* Laura Templeton with 30 Second Success.

Starting with a Question Example:

> *Does anyone here ever feel like running from the room or throwing up when it's your turn to give your thirty-second message? (Raise hand)* At 30 Second Success, we provide business owners and professionals with a branded thirty-second message that they deliver with clarity and confidence. *"Ditch the Pitch & Start Connecting!"™ Schedule an appointment today.* Laura Templeton, CEO of 30 Second Success.

Telling a Story Example:

> *I have a client who would hide in the Ladies Room when it was time for thirty-second messages because of her fear. Imagine how many opportunities she missed.* While working together, I was able to provide her with a clear, concise message she now delivers with confidence and a smile! *If you know someone missing out on business, see me today. Laura Templeton with 30 Second Success.*

This is the simple formula in action. Clear, concise, and confident messaging matters the most. Keeping your message to four to five concise sentences at most will ensure that you stay well within the thirty-second window. Doing so will make you look like the expert you are.

> *Staying within thirty seconds makes you look like the expert you are.*

Remember these key components of The Formula:

1. **Pain Point**. What's the pain or problem your ideal clients' experience? Express it as a question, statement, or story. Connect with the emotion attached to the pain or problem. How do they feel?

2. **Solution**. How do you solve their problem? Be distinctive, stand out, and be different. What sets you apart from the other people in your field…share that!

3. **Call-to-Action**. Now that you've told them they have a problem and why you are the person to solve it for them, what do you want them to do with that information? Make sure your call to action is a commanding statement.

4. **Identify a Good Referral (Optional)**. Reiterate your pain point here.

5. **Who You Are.** *Always* end with your name and company. Even if you get buzzed, state your name and company as you are sitting down. You've got their attention, allow them to write down who, and why they want to follow up with you.

> *Four or five clear, concise sentences delivered with confidence makes you look like an expert.*

To reiterate, keeping your message to four to five clear, concise sentences makes a great impression. Keeping it at or slightly under thirty seconds shows respect to the other people in the room and conveys that you are confident in what you do. If you've ever been in a situation where someone tends to drone on or becomes embarrassed by getting dinged by the thirty-second timer, you understand what I am saying.

Take the notes you created when we reviewed each of the key components and put your message together. Pick one great line from each key element, massage it to make sure it is clear and concise, then write it down. This is your first draft. It may take a few tries before you really like it and start to feel comfortable. The important thing is to be flexible and creative. Remember that it is about connecting with your words.

What's going to connect with your audience on an emotional level? What's going to make them feel the pain? Speak to the "emotional state" of your ideal client you identified earlier and look up some of the words that express that state and use them when describing the pain or problem they have. Think about what you need to say that will make your ideal client sit up and take notice? What's going to make them want to know more? Write it down!

✎ **At this point, pause, look over your notes and put your thirty-second message together.**

Get Feedback

Practice and time yourself as you deliver your thirty-second message. When practicing, ask someone you trust to be your audience and ask them to give you some honest feedback. Don't be afraid to ask for advice and edit your message until you are comfortable and confident that it will resonate with your ideal clients.

Many people like to speak "off the cuff" and dislike or struggle with memorization. That's where being a great storyteller comes in, but you must remember to be short and sweet if you only have thirty seconds... what's the pain, how did you solve the problem, what do you want them to do, who you are. Four to five sentences maximum will keep you within the allotted time.

I have an amazing client who is a Feng Shui consultant. She was one of my very first clients, and we had several sessions to work on re-writing her messaging because, in her words, "it didn't feel right" any longer. What we discovered was that her creative soul needed the freedom to express itself in the moment. We also realized she is a great storyteller.

With some additional coaching and a deeper understanding of the formula, she now tells stories about her clients and how she helps them clear their blocks with her services and classes. Telling stories connects with her creative soul, and sticking with the formula keeps her from going into deep detail by giving people just enough information to pique their curiosity and want to know more.

Getting feedback from people you trust to be honest and truthful is very helpful. When you have people you trust around you, they want to see you succeed and are honored that you ask for their feedback. Your network is there for you, and if they aren't, it might be time for a new network.

As an added bonus for purchasing this book, you are invited to join this private Facebook group:

30 Second Connect with 30 Second Success
(https://facebook.com/groups/30SecondConnect/)

Ask to join the group and answer a few key questions to gain access. Have your book receipt for reference or tell us who gifted you with it. The Facebook group is a safe space to share your thirty-second message and receive feedback from other members with the purposeful intention of helping one another.

Common Questions

You now have the basic thirty-second message formula: what's their pain, how do you solve their problem, your call to action, and who you are. Here are some common questions I receive, along with examples of how to overcome them. If you have additional questions of your own, feel free to post them in the Facebook group (https://facebook.com/groups/30SecondConnect/).

How do I shorten my message?

Sometimes we don't even get thirty seconds, we may only get ten or twenty seconds.

To make your message shorter, drop the pain points. Use only your solution, a brief call to action, and your name and company. This is why your solution needs to be just as strong as your pain statement. You've got to capture their attention.

Example:

Corporate event planners hire me to deliver interactive workshops on crafting your thirty-second message and connecting with your network. Schedule me for your next event. Laura Templeton with 30 Second Success.

Sometimes, for various reasons, we don't even get ten or twenty seconds, and you are told to give only your name and company. I encourage you to use your name, company, *and* tagline in this situation (I'm a little rebellious when it comes to coloring inside the lines on this one). Your tagline will still resonate with people in the audience and create curiosity. After all, we are there to connect, right?

Example:

> *I'm Laura Templeton, with 30 Second Success, helping you "Ditch the Pitch and Start Connecting!"*™

How do I lengthen my message?

To lengthen…become a great storyteller! We all know great stories. Use one of yours or someone else's. People remember stories; in fact, people will remember a story before they will remember a detail that isn't connected to one.

Example:

> *Most people struggle to communicate who they are in thirty seconds or less; for some, it may even cause gripping fear. I have a client who used to go to the ladies' room when it was time for thirty-second messages, and she'd leave before the meetings were over. She missed out on numerous opportunities to connect for more than a year until we were finally introduced. After working together to give her a great message, tools to deliver it with confidence, and the skills to connect with her network, she now looks forward to meetings. If you know someone who avoids networking, so they don't have to give a thirty-second message, introduce us today. Laura Templeton with 30 Second Success.*

What if I have more than one business?

Many people with more than one business struggle to put them together in one message without going over thirty seconds. Here are some suggestions that you will find helpful.

- ✧ Find the common thread if there is one. Perhaps your businesses are connected in some way. Think about it, some people have more than one business that has to do with fashion or health products.

- ✧ Sometimes they may not have anything in common. That's okay too. Don't be afraid to combine business or services by being creative and having fun with it. This can bring extra attention to your message.

Example: something in common (*Pain-Solution-Call-Who*):

Most people struggle with clarity of mind and speech. I help people get clear through their senses and their words. If you're ready to lift the brain fog and connect with your words, schedule a call with me today. Laura Templeton bringing you essential oils and 30 Second Success.

Sometimes they may not have anything in common, or so one would think. Use your solutions for both businesses.

Example: nothing in common (*Solution-Solution-Call-Who*):

As a certified archery instructor, I teach people of all ages and levels proper technique. As a thirty-second message coach, I help people make an impact with their words. If you're ready to hit a bullseye every time, schedule a call with me today. Laura Templeton with Templeton Archery Pros and 30 Second Success.

When combining businesses, it is easier to start with a statement rather than a question. When combining the two, be careful to use **"and"** <u>not</u> **"also."** "Also" is one of those words in the English language that has a negative effect. It actually causes the brain to cancel out anything you said before it. People will focus on whatever you say AFTER the word "also."

Example:

"I am a thirty-second message coach, and an archery instructor" is more memorable than "I am a thirty-second message coach, and I'm also an archery instructor." You want to be known as "this AND this," not just "this." AND is a connecting word—use it.

(Truth be told, I am the 30 Second Success coach, and for fun and relaxation, my husband and I enjoy shooting and teaching archery, but I don't typically promote archery, at least not at this time. The above statements are for example purposes.)

How do I change it up?

This is a great question that deserves a chapter of its very own. There are plenty of creative ways to change up your message once you have that true go to message that you can deliver with confidence anytime the opportunity presents itself.

I hear this quite often from clients who network with the same people each and every week:

✧   *They all know what I do!*

✧   *I feel like I'm saying the same old boring thing!*

✧   *How do I change it up?*

They worry that people aren't listening because they've heard it all before. Truth is, we get bored with our own commercials sometimes, too.

It's okay to change it up and keep it interesting. BUT...you need to be good at it, and you need to think it through ahead of time. Don't try and do it on the spot; there are people, people with lots of networking experience, who can pull this off successfully, but I don't recommend it.

Change the Pain Point

The easiest way to change up your message is to address the different pain points your ideal client experiences. The rest of your message—how you solve their problem, your call to action, and who you are—can stay exactly the same, making this one of the most common ways to change your message.

Here are some things you can address simply by changing the pain point:

- ✧ Benefits

- ✧ Seasonal Offerings

- ✧ Other Services

- ✧ Various Products

Examples:

Option 1: *Most people struggle to effectively communicate who they are in thirty seconds or less. I help people develop their thirty-second message for networking and video. If you're ready to "Ditch the Pitch and Start Connecting," schedule a call today. Laura Templeton, 30 Second Success.*

Option 2: *Business owners avoid networking because they don't know what to share. I help people develop their thirty-second message for networking and video. If you're ready to "Ditch the Pitch and Start Connecting," schedule a call today. Laura Templeton, 30 Second Success.*

Here's another example:

Option 1: *Is your holiday gift list ready, or are you one of those last-minute buyers? Avoid the stress of shopping and schedule all of your gift-giving with us. We'll buy it, wrap it, and deliver it while keeping your budget intact. Make a great impression on your personal and professional list, call us today. Carol, with Gift Impressions by Carol.*

Option 2: *Wedding season and graduations are right around the corner? Avoid the stress of shopping and schedule all of your gift-giving with us. We'll buy it, wrap it, and deliver it while keeping your budget intact. Make a great impression on your personal and professional list, call us today. Carol, with Gift Impressions by Carol.*

Playing off your audience

Think of your audience. Who are your power partners in the room? Who do you want to give a little shout out to? Trust me, people really appreciate it when you mention them in your commercial. Who can you bounce off of? When I say "bounce," it's more like who can you connect your services to? By enhancing what they mention, you educate people on how they would benefit from working with both of you.

Who has a similar client base that you can piggyback off of their commercial and at the same time, elevate them? By elevating them and their services, you build credibility with the audience and your power partners and encourage more referrals for both of you by doing so. This is where understanding your ideal clients and the people who serve them (your power partners) really comes in handy.

Think about the people in your group that you would consider great referral sources or power partners. For a realtor, it might be a home appraiser or mortgage loan officer. For a builder, it might be a roofer or flooring contractor. Listen to them as they go before you and key in on something they typically say about a job or client. For me, it might be a videographer or web designer who just mentioned how they serve clients.

Example:

As Josh just mentioned, adding videos to your website can greatly improve your SEO. I help clients with their thirty-second messaging to maximize their impact. If you're ready to increase your SEO ranking with video, schedule a call with me today. Laura Templeton with 30 Second Success.

Get Creative

You have lots of options, and your creativity is limitless once you have a deep understanding of your core message and how the simple formula works. Once you do understand, and once you have that foundational message down pat, you can get really creative. Have fun and play with your message. A word of caution here: be careful not to stray too far from your original message, or you might confuse your audience.

> *Once you have your "go-to message" you can play and have fun.*

Try some of these options.

Lead with a question

Invite interaction by leading with a question. Questions are a great way to change up your message. You can come up with several different questions, and the rest of your message can stay the same. Think about it, how you serve your clients stays the same even if you have multiple services you offer because your ideal client stays the same.

Remember what I shared earlier? Don't forget to raise your hand and pay attention to who responds. This is a great way to identify who you need to follow up with. Below you'll see examples of messages with only the question changed.

Examples:

Who struggles with what to say when it comes to your thirty-second message? (Raise your hand.) *I help you develop your thirty-second messages for networking and video that resonates with your audience and drives business to your door. If you're ready to make an impact with your words in thirty seconds or less, schedule a call with me today. Laura Templeton with 30 Second Success.*

How many of you feel that it's a struggle to effectively communicate your message? (Raise your hand.) *I help you develop your thirty-second messages for networking and video that resonates with your audience and drives business to your door. If you're ready to make an impact with your words in thirty seconds or less, schedule a call with me today. Laura Templeton with 30 Second Success.*

How many of you want to create impactful videos but don't know what to say? (Raise your hand.) *I help you develop your thirty-second messages for networking and video that resonates with your audience and drives business to your door. If you're ready to make an impact with your words in thirty seconds or less, schedule a call with me today. Laura Templeton with 30 Second Success.*

Use Visuals

Visuals, like stories, create an immediate connection with your audience. When you have a product or an image, you can physically show or pass around, people pay more attention. Visuals are memorable and effective because they help people process, understand, and retain more information more quickly.

A 2013 article published by *Science Daily*[7] referencing research from the University of California, Davis, shows how visual attention affects activity in specific brain cells. The paper published in the journal *Nature*, shows that visual attention increases the efficiency of signaling into the brain's cerebral cortex and boosts the ratio of signal over noise. So it is safe to assume, and I am sure we've all experienced this first-hand, that visuals grab attention and quiet the surrounding noise which in turn helps us focus.

Visuals are a great way to break through all the noise, and they help your audience focus. Be mindful of the visuals you share and how they relate to your message by considering how your audience will receive them.

Recently a jeweler in my network gave a quick five-minute presentation. During his presentation, he talked about identifying a diamond, the different types, sizes, colors, clarity, etc. He passed around simple visual handouts that supported the information he was sharing.

As he closed his presentation, he passed out envelopes to everyone. He explained that they had done a recent marketing promotion and had passed out 500 envelopes: 494 contained cubic zirconias, and six contained real diamonds. As he passed out envelopes, he said he would tell us how to determine what stone we'd received. The room grew quiet, and the excitement was palpable. Once everyone had their envelopes, he told us to read the label for where to take the stone to find out what we had. Great marketing, right? But the simplicity of that little white envelope was all he needed to hook everyone in the room. Hats off to him!

Here are some suggestions that might lead you to a creative idea of your own.

Types of Visuals

- ✧ Before-and-After Photos. Personal or client photos are powerful for a weight loss or fitness coach.

- ✧ Clothing and accessories. Wear them!

- ✧ A document. A CPA client holds up a letter from the IRS and tells a story about how he was able to provide documentation and save his client from having to pay thousands to the IRS)

- ✧ Sold sign. One of my real estate clients holds up a sold sign and shares her "Days on Market" stats.

- ✧ Product samples. Offer a limited quantity to the first few people to see you at the end of the meeting.

- ✧ Marketing materials. These make great giveaways.

Example:

Most people dread hearing the buzzer (hold up your phone) *before they finish talking. At 30 Second Success, we teach you how to create a message that replaces fear with confidence. If you're ready to make an impact with your words in thirty seconds or less, sign up for a workshop today. Laura Templeton with 30 Second Success.*

Another really fun thing to do is to ask for audience participation. I know a lovely woman who sells Ruby Ribbon, a clothing line that has changed the face of the undergarment industry. Every time she does her thirty-second commercial, at least one person will stand up and flash the audience with their camisole. (Good thing she networks with women!)

A word of advice…keep it simple and engaging, but be careful not to get distracted by your visuals. If you fidget and fumble with things you want to hold up, that's just too distracting for your audience. If it isn't simple and easy, don't do it. Don't set yourself up for an epic fail. Better to be empty-handed than to look overly awkward or confused. Remember that clear, concise, and confident is how you want to come across to your audience.

Wear Your Brand

There are a couple ways to wear your brand. Choose one or choose them all, but make it a conscious effort to wear your brand. This helps people identify you quickly when you stand out. It also expresses a certain level of professionalism people appreciate.

✦ *Wear Your Apparel*

Have branded apparel? WEAR IT! Wearing your "swag" (as we loving refer to it) definitely attracts attention. I recently wore a shirt with one of my client's brand logos on it and had someone ask me what it was when I was standing in the checkout line at the store. Logo wear is inexpensive advertising, and the visual impact is amazing. Just by wearing, you are opening yourself up to business opportunities wherever you go.

✦ *Wear Your Name Tag*

If you don't have branded apparel, get the next best thing, name tags made with your company logo, and your name on them. I have two. One to keep in my bag and one for in my car. These are more professional than the ones handed out at meetings, and you can get magnetic ones for a low cost online. Wearing your logo attracts attention, creates curiosity, and adds a level of professionalism to your presentation.

I feel compelled to add a little blurb about name tag etiquette here. Always wear it on the right side of your chest with the center in line with your armpit or slightly higher depending on the size. When you shake hands (etiquette dictates that this should be your right hand), the eyes of the person you are meeting will be drawn to your name and then to your eyes. Eye contact is crucial when meeting someone for the first time, or any time for that matter.

Mary Kay Cosmetics trains their representatives to do this, and it really works. I truly believe everyone should learn this tip, especially women who feel compelled to place their name tags in the middle of their blouse or low on their hip. Draw attention to your eyes, not elsewhere. Invest in a magnetic name tag and never worry about those sticky "my name is..." tags getting lost or caught in your hair again.

✧ *Wear Your Colors*

Another way to wear your brand is to incorporate your company colors into your wardrobe. Years ago, at a branding conference, they shared how important it is to show up as part of your brand. Your physical appearance matters to first impressions and all that, and we'll get into that a little deeper elsewhere, but here I want to touch on the premise of wearing your brand.

I get it if your company colors aren't your favorite, but consider slight changes of shade that might be better for you, it doesn't have to be exact. Wear your brand colors when you are out doing company business. Perhaps create a "uniform" of sorts to make it easier to get into your brand when you're getting ready. This has actually been a Godsend for me when getting ready for early morning meetings. You'd be surprised by how many people are in tune with what you wear and how those colors make an impact when they look at your online presence. As my photographer says, "You are your brand." Wearing your brand is just one more way for people to associate you with the brand image you want them to remember.

30 Second Success Quick Tips

Create curiosity, compel your audience to want more.

The important thing is to have fun with your message! You don't have to be serious all the time. Even a mortician can be light and entertaining when it comes to their thirty-second message. The funeral business is a serious business, but breaking the ice with a light-hearted confident message can open doors and create a comfort level. Remember, your message is about reaching the emotion associated with your ideal client's problem and being the solution they may not yet realize they need.

Once you have your listener's attention, you can transition to one-on-one meetings and creating deeper connections. In part two you will gain a better understanding of the networking principles, building strong referral relationships, and developing power partners. So keep reading!

Keep your message to four to five sentences at most.

This is worth repeating, especially for storytellers. Short and concise is best. When you keep your message to four to five clear, concise sentences that really bring your point across, you will be surprised at how easy it is to finish within thirty seconds. By keeping your message short, people really notice; this lends more credibility to your presentation, sets you apart as an expert, expresses respect for the facilitator and the other people in the room, and feels great! It also makes it easier to remember.

Practice at home in front of a mirror or camera and time yourself.

Practice is crucial! Practice helps you find your comfort zone, helps you create the right tone, inflection, and body language that effectively communicate your message. I still practice my thirty-second message in the car while driving to business events. I find that when I practice on the way, once I get there, I can focus on the other people in the room, and when it's my turn, I already know what I am going to say, and it flows well.

> It takes less than eight seconds for someone to decide if what you have to say is worth listening to. Make those first seconds count!

Use a timer when you practice. Sometimes we try to add a little extra here and there as we practice, pushing us just slightly beyond the thirty seconds. Using a timer will help you stay on track and gain confidence along the way, giving you that "I've got this!" feeling.

Delivering with Confidence

Once you know what you are going to say, you need the tools to deliver it with confidence. Yes, having the right message is one of those tools. But, there are a few additional tools you need to deliver your message effectively and connect with your audience. Here are a few simple strategies to help you do just that.

- ✧ **Stand up even if no one else does**. Standing up gives you a sense of control and gets people to look in your direction. When you stand up, all eyes should be on you, and you have a better view of the people on the opposite side of the room.

- ✧ **Choose your seat wisely**. Sit on the perimeter of the room to have a better view and to give people a better view of you. This may not always be possible, especially in smaller rooms. Pick a seat close to the front where you can move about easily.

- ✧ **Improve your view**. If you can't see everyone, move to the front of the room or to an outside wall where you can see the whole room. Try to avoid having your back to anyone. Again this isn't always possible, so if you need to, decide on the best direction to face when giving your message and avoid spinning around.

- **Connect with friendly faces**. This really helps calm the nerves. You don't have to "look" at everyone in the room, but making eye contact with the people you feel most comfortable with or who seem the most friendly helps.

- **Look to the leaders**. Networking leaders want success for everyone who attends their meetings. They have a vested interest in helping you feel welcome and comfortable. They are also great connectors, so focusing on sharing your message with them will help them know who to introduce you to.

- **Avoid cue cards**. They are distracting, and most people have a tendency to read from them and not look at their audience. The best way to avoid them is to know your message. If you feel you need something to keep you on track or if you are someone who likes to be creative on the spot, create a card with the formula written on it. These four points are all you need to keep you on track.

  1. Pain

  2. Solution

  3. Call-to-Action

  4. YOU!

- **Project your voice**. Another great reason to stand up is that it gives you the ability to project your voice by opening up your diaphragm. Make your voice bigger rather than just louder by breathing properly and filling your lungs all the way to the bottom. Your voice will carry better and have a richer, more pleasing sound.

✧ **Articulate with energy to carry your voice**. Most people have rather lazy diction (myself included). You need to articulate clearly and use energy to create clear, crisp consonants. How well you articulate your words impacts how far your voice carries.

✧ **Make your voice bigger, not louder**. Try this exercise: Instead of pushing, imagine that the inside of your throat and mouth is large, as large as the room you're speaking in. That will cause all the muscles around the inside of your throat to pull away, just as they do when you are yawning. The bigger the space inside, the bigger the voice outside.

✧ **Deal with the butterflies**. Recognize that butterflies are nothing more than excited energy, and everyone in the room is feeling that way, too. I am forever grateful to my choir and ballet teachers who taught me that butterflies are nothing more than my excited energy mixed with the energy of the other performers and the audience coming together in anticipation of a great show. When you flip the switch from telling yourself that "it's nerves" to "it's excitement," you get really jazzed to get on with the show.

The real key to your success is to get out there and practice. The more you network, the more often you share your message, the more comfortable and confident you will become. Soon the butterflies in your stomach will begin to get you excited rather than making you want to run and hide.

Understand Your Audience

This is another area I like to explore with clients. Think about where you're meeting your clients right now. Are you networking already? Where are you meeting your potential clients? Where are you meeting people who may know your potential clients?

Understanding who it is you are presenting to will help you develop a message that will speak to their hearts more readily. Think about it, networking with a group of women versus a mixed group is very different, just like networking with a group of start-ups is different from networking with established business owners and professionals.

Tailoring your specific message to your audience makes it easier to connect. This happens when you know your audience and make a few tweaks to your message that are more meaningful to them. For example, you would address a group of start-ups slightly differently than you would address a group of established business owners.

✐ **Write down every place you network or where you connect with your ideal clients currently.**

Time for a Rewrite

Now that you know the formula and how to deliver your thirty-second message with confidence, ✐ rewrite your message once again and tailor it for your ideal client. Get creative, but be very intentional about what you want them to do now that they know they need you.

Here's how I'd rewrite Mary's message (you remember Mary from the beginning of the book, right?):

Mary's Original Message:

Uh, hi. I'm Mary Smith. I'm a photographer. Uh, I do family portraits, newborn babies, weddings, life events, uh, headshots, oh, and product photos. My studio is located at 4112 Sunny Lane, two miles down the road from here. Uh, I can take pictures inside or outside. My prices are very reasonable. Uh, you can buy a package of images or pick the ones you want, à la carte. When you're ready to schedule your session, call me. Thank you.

Mary's new message following the formula:

Children grow, people pass, but time continues on. When you experience an image of your children playing in the park or your grandparents' anniversary (hold up a photo), your soul stirs with emotion, and love and warmth flood your heart. I capture treasured moments for families to hold onto. Cherished moments are meant to live on your walls, not on your computer. Schedule a session today. Mary Smith, Sunny Lane Photography.

Your message is about connecting with your audience by connecting with their emotions, with their hearts, and getting them to want to know more.

PART TWO

What is Networking, REALLY?

You have your thirty-second message nailed, so now it's time to learn how to maximize your networking efforts, build better connections, and ultimately increase your business and your income.

Networking, a noun, defined as: **"the action or process of interacting with others to exchange information and develop professional or social contacts,"** according to Oxford. No matter how you define it, networking is one of the best ways to make trusted business connections and develop strong relationships with people you will do business with for years to come.

Networking takes a lot of the guesswork out of who to hire when you need help because you've built trust with your network, and you know who your "go-to" people are. Likewise, they will gladly use your services and refer you to their extended network of friends, family, associates, and acquaintances based on this level of trust.

> *For someone to recommend you, they must feel comfortable enough to put their own reputation behind your work.*

Networking truly is about connecting and developing the **know, like, and trust** factor. Networking and referral expert Bob Burg, the author of *Endless Referrals*[8], is famous for his quote, "All things being equal, people do business with, and refer business to people they know, like, and trust." The best approach to networking is to determine that you will build a foundation of trust among the people in your network by forging relationships with them.

Ultimately, networking is about business when you do it well and with the right attitude. Building relationships takes time. If you are willing to invest the time, the rewards are well worth it!

> *Networking is about relationships—not selling!*

Networking is about:

- ❖ **Building Relationships.** Getting to know the people in your network. Understanding how you can help one another. Getting comfortable with the people you surround yourself with regularly.

- ❖ **Building Credibility.** Showing up, doing what you say you will do when you say you will do it, and supporting the people you network with regularly builds credibility. People watch how you interact and look for you to be genuine.

- ❖ **Developing the *Know, Like, and Trust Factor.*** People get to know you, they see how you interact with others, and they listen to what other members have to say about you. This helps them decide if you are someone they want to know, they actually like, and that they trust with their business and/or their people.

- ❖ **Developing Long Term Referral Partners.** Once they get to know you, they start to understand who it is they want to connect you with. If you serve the same or similar clients, they need to know you will treat them well. This knowledge comes through time and trust.

✦ **Making Connections On an Emotional Level.** People want to know the people in their network. It's not just what you do but who you are. This comes through time and trust as well, time well spent getting to know your network and letting them get to know you.

Word-of-Mouth Marketing

The most effective form of marketing is influencer marketing, otherwise known as word-of-mouth marketing. When you get people talking positively about you and recommending you to other people, you've obviously made a good impression.

Networking meetings and events are the best places to form those relationships and to help people gain a better understanding of who you are. Become memorable, make a good impression, stay connected, and help them feel confident enough to hire or recommend you.

Two Types of Networking

✦ In-person

✦ Online

While I will focus primarily on in-person networking, most of what I share in this chapter can be adapted for online networking. Personally, I love the personal contact at networking events, and I really enjoy meeting new and interesting people. Much of my inspiration and ideas come from the people I meet. So you'll definitely see more emphasis on in-person networking in this book.

You can hire social media experts to help you become excellent in the online space, or who can do it for you, but in-person networking you need to do yourself. I know some people hire people to handle their business development, but ultimately they still need to connect with their network to build relationships with the people they serve.

However, you decide to network, in-person, online, or outsourced, here are some "How-Tos" to help you get better results.

In-person networking offers many different types of networking opportunities to choose from:

◇ **Networking Organizations.** Networking groups form to connect and create community. These groups bring an educational component to their meetings to support their membership.

◇ **Referral Networking.** Networking with specific guidelines, most times only allowing one business per industry to attend, to pass valid income-producing referrals to one another.

◇ **Business Card Exchanges**. Open networking events where multiple conversations take place, business cards are exchanged, and follow up takes place afterward.

◇ **Speed Networking**. Similar to speed dating, where you have one-to-two minutes to sit across from someone and give them your message and answer a few brief questions. Events are well organized and timed, follow up takes place afterward.

◇ **Happy Hour Networking**. Similar to business card exchanges but in a more relaxed environment allowing for longer, more casual conversations, follow up takes place afterward.

◇ **Business Roundtable Networking**. Industry or service area-specific meetings designed to bring individuals together who serve the same or a similar community. Open sharing of ideas and support is the focus.

✧ **Community Events and Outings**. Both public and private, these offer many networking opportunities in a more casual atmosphere.

✧ **Association Networking**. Industry-specific associations organize different types of networking events to support folks in their industry through education, support, and connection.

There are many options to choose from. Take your time and learn about the different options or try something different if you've been networking at the same place for a while. Variety offers more opportunities to connect and grow.

Face-to-Face Networking

In-person networking has been around since the early days of commerce. It's how business owners did business together. It's how they found out about other opportunities and people who they could collaborate with on projects. It's how people found the contractor from the next town that came and built their porch.

The places where we network may have changed, but the fundamental way in which we connect hasn't changed. Why should it? It works! Meeting people in-person cuts out a lot of angst when hiring people if you already know them or have a recommendation from someone you trust. It actually makes me a little sad when I meet people who don't like networking. Most of the time, it's because they've never tried it or they're afraid to give their thirty-second message because they hate public speaking. We've already addressed that in this book—so, no more excuses!

How you show up speaks volumes and cuts out a lot of wasted time

> How you show up speaks volumes about you.

back and forth with phone calls and emails. When you spend time with people, they pick up on much more than your words. Here are the cues they are looking for to help them decide if you are someone they want to know:

- ✧ **Body language.** Are you open and inviting or closed off and withdrawn?

- ✧ **Interaction with others.** Do you play nicely with others?

- ✧ **How you treat people.** Are you kind, considerate, and likable?

- ✧ **How you pay attention.** Are you a good listener?

- ✧ **How you talk.** Do you talk at or talk to people?

- ✧ **Your heart attitude.** Are you genuine?

- ✧ **Sticking power.** Are you here to stay or just visiting?

- ✧ **Play nicely with others.** Are you personable?

- ✧ **Acting in their best interest.** Can they know, like, and trust you?

All of these things become evident more quickly when you spend time with people. They want to know if you are the type of person that shows up with good intentions every time or if you are going to flake out. They want to know that you can be trusted to be there for them when they or someone they know needs you.

Where to Network

How do you decide? "Try it before you…buy it!" I'm sure you've heard that one before. Well, it applies here too. Try the different types of networking to see what you enjoy the most, is it the learnings, the connecting, or the happy hour aspect that is most attractive to you.

Another great practice is to go where the people you know go. Let's edit that slightly for a different twist. Go where the people you want to

> *Go where the people you want to get to know go.*

get to know go. Because frankly, networking is about getting to know people and connecting with new people...

- ✧ Ask your peers and mentors where they network and if it would be a good group for you.

- ✧ Ask your clients where they like to connect with people in their industry and if you could tag along sometime.

- ✧ Look online. Meetup.com and Facebook are great places to find networking groups in your local community and online.

- ✧ Visit your local Chamber of Commerce. Chambers have many activities and active members. Consider joining more than one chamber if your network is in more than one coverage area.

- ✧ Ask your network. It never hurts to put it out to your current network. Ask the people you are connected with what networks they belong to and what they like about them. Ask if you can join them sometime.

- ✧ If your ideal clients are all within a certain geographic area, go there. If you live in a suburb of a large city and most of your clients are in the city, it makes sense to network in the city.

- ✧ If you are new to the area, ask around. Ask your local store owners, many communities have a Business Owners Association, start there.

Ask the people you *know, like, and trust*! Then ask them for an invite if they haven't already extended one. It's always more comfortable to network with a friend, or at least someone you know!

I have found that there are a lot of women's organizations in my region. I love to connect, so I've selected three organizations in different counties. All of them present me with great opportunities to connect with people from different industries, professions, and organizations.

I have several clients who have found that they were networking with people who they absolutely enjoyed but were not their ideal clients. After going through the exercise of identifying their ideal client discussed in an earlier chapter, we were able to help refocus their search for networking groups that were a much better fit.

Effective networking starts with a commitment to showing up. Select one or two networking groups to try, decide which ones work best for you, and then show up consistently.

Pick A Place to Start

You don't have to be in all places. Try a few and find two or three that resonate with you.

Ideally, you want to find groups that are well attended with enough people in the group to connect with and build relationships. Look for groups that have twenty or more members and show consistent growth. It's nice to see new faces at every meeting.

The key to finding a group is trusting your gut and your network. Trust your gut to tell you that these are the people you really want to spend time with and trust your network to help you find the group that will help you grow both personally and professionally.

Once You've Landed Somewhere

Give it a chance. Sometimes it takes twelve-to-eighteen months before your networking efforts begin to see results.

Again, it's about developing that **know, like,** and **trust** factor (Are we starting to see a pattern here?) and teaching people who and how to refer you. Consistency and reliability will help to shorten that window of development.

Be Willing to Serve

- ✧ **Offer help** – Not necessarily to run things, unless of course, you want to.

- ✧ **Volunteer without the obligation** – It's a choice, extra hands are always welcome when available.

- ✧ **Show up early and stay late** – Be the memorable face in the group.

- ✧ **Greet people as they arrive** – Be the unofficial greeter.

- ✧ **Invite new people to sit with you if they are alone** – A lot of people are uncomfortable the first time they visit. Make them feel welcome, and they'll come back.

> *Networking continues long after the meeting is over.*

Introduce others and invite them into your conversation – When someone new shows up, invite them in. When someone interrupts to say hello, introduce them, and continue your conversation.

Lead with a heart of service, and you will never go wrong. Put the interest of your group and the other members of your group first, and you will always come out a winner.

Networking Best Practices

Conveying confidence is critical! If you want to be taken seriously, be professional.

Show up and be heard. What you do is important, people need to hear what you have to say. Unfortunately, they will see you first, so be sure that your outward appearance matches the message you want to share. Project confidence – be warm, friendly, and inviting not just with your voice, but with your presence and the way you carry yourself.

> *Show up and be heard.*

Appearance

> *Check the mirror one last time.*

Stop in the bathroom, and be sure to check your appearance one last time. Who knows what the humidity has done to your hair or that your shirt has come untucked (if you don't prefer to wear it that way) in the twenty minutes since you've left home.

Smooth out the wrinkles in your suit, freshen up your lipstick if you wear it, and be sure to check for toilet paper on your shoe (yes, my biggest fear before giving a presentation, and it actually happened.) I had a client who used to show up all wrinkled like she had just rolled out of bed. It was a hard conversation to have with her, but it has made a difference since she invested in a steamer.

Be sure to check your breath too. Nothing is more offensive than a bad case of morning breath, even when you try to cover it with coffee. Carry something to freshen your breath with you at all times. The people you greet will appreciate the consideration.

Body Language

Folding your arms across your chest is a protective mechanism, it also sends a signal that you are closed off from meeting people. Be careful of the messages you send with your facial expressions as well. When your eyes start to wander, or your smile turns upside down (unless they are telling you something sad), people begin to think you are unapproachable. Be engaging by asking questions and truly listening for the answers.

Be open and welcoming. Extend your hand in a warm, friendly hand-shake and smile a genuine friendly smile. Fidgeting around or looking for an escape route sends a really bad signal. Even if you are waiting for someone you need to talk to show up, give the person in front of you your undivided attention. Treat them as if they are the only person in the room. Remain approachable enough for others to want to join the conversation, this will allow you to extract yourself and move to another conversation.

Be open.

Speak Up

People need to hear what you have to say. Engage as many people in conversation as possible during your time together. Get to know new people and expand your network. Connect with the people you planned to meet and have a conversation, even a brief one, to tell them why you wanted to meet and ask for an appointment.

If you have a low voice, do what my client does, preface your message with a quick reference to your inability to talk loud, and people

88

will lean in to hear you. Surprisingly enough, this really gets people to pay attention to what she has to say.

Speak clearly and with authority. You know your business like no one else does, speak with confidence, and if you are unsure of something, offer to get back to them with an answer. This is a great opportunity to follow up.

Be Warm and Inviting

Here's a scenario to think about: You show up at an event you have two choices...There are two people you notice right away. One whom you just saw introduce a new person to three other members and now has two other people waiting to greet him when he is finished with introductions, or the second person who seems to have someone cornered as he tells them all about himself and you notice other people appear to be avoiding him.

Which person do you want to talk to? More importantly, which person do you want to be, the person people look forward to greeting, or the one people avoid?

Be the person people gravitate to. Greet everyone with a warm, inviting smile and a handshake. Ask how they are or about a major life event they may have spoken

> *Be the person people gravitate to.*

about or shared on social media or during a recent conversation.

Tell people you are happy to see them. Make them feel good! Building relationships is about being genuine, showing true interest, and taking part in each other's lives, no matter how brief your time together is. People are attracted to warm, friendly people in the room.

How you make them feel with your warm, inviting tone, your open, friendly posture, and your beautiful smile will make them want to know you. This is the beginning of a beautiful relationship for certain.

Networking is about Relationship Building First and Foremost

Invest the time and make it about THEM. Be purposeful in developing mutually beneficial relationships. It's not always about business, but in many ways, it is the best starting point for building a relationship as you uncover the synergy between you and your network.

> *Make it about them.*

Two simple questions you can ask someone you have met with, like, and feel you could confidently tell others about would be:

1. Who would be a good referral for you?

2. What would you like me to say about you and your business?

Most likely, they will ask you the same questions. (If they don't, you might reconsider the following until you get to know them a little better.) Then keep your eyes and ears open for people who need their services, and they will, in turn, do the same.

Business Comes as a Result of Your Efforts

When you work at building relationships and giving good referrals, people do the same for you. They want to respond in kind as a way of thanking you. It's how most people are built.

Be careful not to expect or demand the same in response, that's not how relationships work. Sometimes they aren't equal.

There is a woman whom I've networked with for years. I sent several clients to her that absolutely loved working with her over the years, but until recently, I hadn't received one referral from her. The timing and the need were right when she thought of me to help one of her major clients with their corporate message.

She felt she could trust me to give them the right guidance and told them as much. When I thanked her, she actually thanked me for never having pressured her for clients even after I had given her so many referrals. She said that was partly how she knew she could trust me to treat her client right.

Some people are naturally more giving than others. They truly grasp the concept of serving. Others need a little guidance, hence asking the two questions and planting the seeds necessary to help your contacts to know how to refer you when the time comes.

Put Your Smile On

Show up with the right attitude and a smile. A warm, friendly, and inviting personality attracts clients and referrals.

> *A warm personality attracts clients and referrals.*

Your posture and appearance matter. If you sit with a scowl on your face and your arms crossed over your chest, that does not say "welcome" at all. You might be giving off the wrong signals unintentionally, so be aware of your appearance. Be friendly and inviting, starting with your smile.

Leave whatever is happening in your life at the door. I know it's hard, and we are often dealing with some seriously big stuff. But, being fully engaged in the group and being totally present and attentive will help you to be more open and inviting to those around you. People see it and are naturally attracted to you.

Consistency Matters

> *Be seen to be heard.*

Showing up consistently builds credibility. People do business with people they know, like, and trust. Attend meetings regularly, so they get to know you, like you, and trust you. To do that, you must show up. Block out the time and commit to it as a non-negotiable, noting that the only way you'd miss a meeting would be due to illness, vacation, or death.

Showing up day after day, week after week, and month after month truly matters to the people in the room. Whether online or in-person, when you stop showing up at first people miss you, then they actually forget you because they think you've forgotten them.

Mark your calendar for the networking groups you've committed to and make them a priority. Be careful not to overbook yourself, you need time for business (you know, those income-producing activities.) If the groups are online, be sure to schedule relevant posts for the group's benefit and interact regularly. Decide what that regular basis is and stick with it.

Step Up to the Microphone

Confidence attracts clients.

By this, I mean, participate. Show up early in-person and online. Greet people as they arrive. Welcome new people and introduce them as others arrive.

Be memorable by being a fan of the group. Share how you have benefited from being a member and express your appreciation for the people in the room. Share testimonials about people you've worked with, received referrals from, or have had a great connection with.

For on-line networking join groups, and be engaging. Share positive helpful information. Comment on other people's posts and participate in live group chats when they are available.

Make Your Referral Partners Feel Heard

Listen to what your referral partners need. It may be something you or one of your other referral partners offer. Position yourself in a way that helps them see that you have a solution for them, even if it's a referral to someone you know, like, and trust. They may become your ideal client or a great referral partner when they understand that you have the knowledge, expertise, and connections to be a resource for them.

When you have an opportunity to share, tell a story. Share a story about success a client, customer, or you yourself have experienced with your product or service. Share in a way that connects with a challenge they mentioned (Remember: what was the problem, how did you solve it). Keep it simple but engaging. Take the opportunity to share in a way that expresses your knowledge and experience.

Be careful not to jump into telling your listeners all about you. Share your story and then turn it back to them. Remember, it's all about them. Make them feel heard by being genuinely interested in what they have to say, not what you have to say.

Be a Good Listener

By now, I know you've read how important it is to "listen" to your audience. Listening is an art that can be mastered with practice. The first step is to be truly interested in what others have to say.

> *Stop waiting for your turn to talk.*

Think of a time when you felt genuinely heard? How did that make you feel? What did you learn from that experience?

✐ **This might be a good time to write and reflect on the emotion that obviously still resonates with your soul.**

Being a good listener doesn't necessarily mean you never get a chance to talk, it just means that you understand the power of having a true conversation. It's about the give and take, or the Four Rs:

1. **Request**: ask a question

2. **Response**: allow time for the answer

3. **Reply**: respond to their follow up question or acknowledge what they said

4. **Repeat**: ask another question

When engaged in networking conversations, it is helpful to remember the Four Rs. Networking conversations are designed to help you get a quick idea of who you're speaking with and if it's someone you'd like to get to know more, especially when speaking with someone you've never met. This is different than one-on-one meeting conversations that we explore deeper in another chapter. One-on-one meetings are about building deep connections.

Make a Good First Impression

First impressions matter!

- ✧ **Lead with a Great Smile.** Happy people attract happy people. Sad and angry faces scare people off.

- ✧ **Have a Firm Handshake.** No wimpy fishy handshakes, this is especially important for women. Extend a firm, not bone-crushing, right-hand while looking them in the eyes and smiling. Be warm and inviting!

- ✧ **Make & Keep Eye Contact.** While in conversation with others, make eye contact as much as possible. This expresses genuine interest. Nothing is more frustrating than when you are in a conversation, and they are looking over your shoulder for their next connection.

- ✧ **Join the Conversation.** If you walk in and someone you want to meet is already in conversation, excuse yourself and ask if you can join in. Same goes if you are in a conversation and someone walks in and looks a little awkward, invite them to join you.

- ✧ **Be Polite and Courteous.** Be considerate of others. Don't corner someone. Take a respectful amount of time, schedule another meeting if you wish to get to know them, and excuse yourself to connect with others.

94

The key thing to remember when working on first impressions is that people are attracted to positive, friendly people.

> *Positive, friendly people attract positive, friendly people.*

Collecting Business Cards

Collecting business cards will get you nowhere if all you do is stick them in your pocket, in a shoebox, or on a pile with no real intent to follow up.

It's not about how many cards you collect, it's about the quality conversations you have before someone feels comfortable giving you their card and asking to follow up later.

What to do with those cards?

- ✧ **Write Notes on the Back**. This shows interest and makes the giver feel special.

- ✧ **Follow Up as Noted.** Be sure to reference the notes on your card, especially if you said you'd send or call them with some information. Most people are surprised when you do.

- ✧ **Ask for Newsletter Permission.** Don't just assume it's okay to add someone to your newsletter, ask if it's okay, then send them an invitation with a link for them to opt-in.

- ✧ **Add to your CRM.** Be sure to note the date, event, and any other memory joggers for later reference.

- ✧ **Give Away.** Don't keep the card, give or send it to someone you think might be a good connection for them.

Follow Up When You Say You Will!

> Follow up when you say you will.

This is a test! People want to know you are true to your word. It's the know, like, and trust factor building up in your favor. Do what you say you will do and do it quickly. Follow up when you say you will. If you receive a connection request from someone else, respond right away.

Market Yourself as a Professional

Business Cards

Personally, I believe business cards are the best investment for your business and the only thing you need when you are starting out. Give them away, leave them places, give some to your referral partners, and always have some with you. You never know when you'll meet someone who wants to exchange cards after you've had an amazing conversation with them.

Invest in eye-catching business cards with or without your photo. Make sure the important information is on the front, and it is easy to read. Quality paper and finish make a huge difference, people will feel and comment on them! Ask for a matte finish on the back and allow some space for people to take notes (I teach clients to do that for an easy recall after a networking event).

Name Badges

Avoid those sticky labels that fall off or look like a child's handwriting in crayon by investing in your own magnetic name badge. Having your own badge shows that you've taken the time to invest in your business. Add your name, company, and logo. Make sure it is large enough for people to read.

Buy two, in case you leave one at home. I purchased two from *NametagCountry.com,* and I keep one in my bag and one in my vehicle. Wear it on your right side…Remember, Mary Kay says to wear it on the right to draw eyes to your face when reaching out to shake hands.

Marketing Materials

It's not necessary to go crazy on marketing materials when you are starting out, but whatever you invest in should be of good quality. Invest in professional printing when creating brochures and flyers. Even if you use Staples for printing, it is light years better than your home printer.

Again, it's the image you are projecting. Print in smaller quantities in the beginning, as you may make adjustments to your services and pricing along the way, and you certainly don't want to invest in a lot of obsolete materials.

Directory Listings – USE THEM!

When you have a directory listing available to you through your network as part of your membership, use it! You've paid for it; it's part of your marketing, and they work. This is just another part of your net-working reach. It blows my mind when I work with clients who have never taken the time to complete their profiles for their networking organizations because they don't know what to say.

Well, I say "No more excuses!" and here's why…I have had several clients find me by searching directories of national networking organiza-tions I belong to. I now have clients that stretch across the United States because of these directory listings and the opportunity to connect with many other members.

Side note…with just one of these clients, my annual member-ship dues are covered for the next three years. Get on it, get found, get clients!

Professional Headshot

Get a professional photo and use it. Your face is like your signature when it comes to being found online. Think of it, as fast as we scroll through our phones, there are certain people that we automatically recognize as their picture flips past at lightning speed.

Your image is part of your brand. I encourage you to have fun with it. Make your image stand out and keep it current. If you get a new hairstyle or change hair color, get an updated photo right away; otherwise, you could probably use the same one for two to three years (but where's the fun in that?).

For my very first headshot for 30 Second Success, I wore a coral-colored jacket because it was one of my company colors. What I did not expect was the amount of attention that would get me and how easy it was to find me in a directory just by my photo. Now I get creative with my photos for that reason, and my photographer is happy to help me.

> *Facial recognition wins every time.*

Company Logo

Upload your company logo when possible. It's the next best thing to your photo for identification when someone is scrolling through a directory. Don't have a logo or don't like your old one...time for a new one!

Your logo needs to be everywhere, including in front of the people you network with. If you have the option to post it on the directory, great, do it! If given a choice for photo or logo, photo wins every time... just sayin'. Facial recognition wins every time.

Company Contact Info

Complete as much of your company contact information in the directory as possible. Check it periodically for accuracy. Nothing is more frustrating than a member forgetting to update their email or phone number in a directory when it changes.

I do have a word of caution for you when it comes to your address. Refrain from adding your home address as your office location. I had a really creepy experience because of this and no longer post it publicly when I can avoid it. Let's just say, I am glad my husband was home when the guy came to my front door. I advise against adding your home address to your business card for the same reason.

Business Description

You can use your thirty-second message as part of your business description. Again, it's the strength of your message. What's the pain your ideal client struggles with, how do you help them, and what should someone do if they are reading this and decide they need your help?

You can expand a little more if you have the room, but be sure to invite them to call or visit your website to schedule an appointment.

Professional Bio

Time to shine here! It's all about you, your accomplishments, your success, and what you're doing to change the world now! Use this space to share your story. Remember, people in your network want to know you, so add a little bit of the personal side too but keep to the 80/20 rule...80% business, 20% personal.

Time to shine!

Example:

Helping people develop their thirty-second message, so they no longer feel like running from the room when it's their turn to talk has become my mission. After watching some of the amazing women I know struggle with their messaging I started sharing what I learned in my 15 years of sales and marketing, then word got out that I was helping people. Now, as an author and speaker for companies and associations around the world, I get to enjoy life helping business owners, professionals, and sales teams "Ditch the Pitch and Start

Connecting"™. In my "we" time, I enjoy teaching archery alongside my husband, whom I've been dating for more than thirty-five years, and I can't wait to share archery with my grandchildren.

Member directories are there to promote members, complete them as soon as possible and keep them up to date. Just like your social media profiles and website, this is another way to drive up your SEO and increase your visibility online. Member directories are a perk of membership, use them. Don't let this precious marketing real estate go to waste.

> *Member directories are a perk of membership, use them.*

How you show up in print is just as important as how you show up in person. Be prepared and professional in all your dealings, and people will want to listen to what you have to say. With the right physical, written, and verbal messages working together, you'll make a much better impression with your network.

Online Networking Considerations

> *You need to be where your audience is showing up, but you don't have to be in all places.*

Showing up online is just as important. Don't know where to start? That's okay, know where your audience is showing up online and start there.

All too often, and just like in-person networking, we try to do everything, and then we do nothing well. Think about the different social media platforms and where your clients are showing up. Are you selling B2B or B2C? Do you have a product with great visuals to share? Are you a service provider?

Show Up Where Your Ideal Clients Are Showing Up

Facebook, LinkedIn, Twitter, Instagram, Pinterest, Etsy...be where they are. Be where they expect you to be. Understanding your ideal clients, their habits, and their interests are key to knowing where they show up and what they are looking for. Spend some time (or hire someone to do it for you) looking at where your clients are, what they are sharing, who they follow, and what groups they like.

If you are trying to connect with a particular client, study their online habits and start showing up there, so your name becomes familiar. I recommend doing this well before you contact them to maximize name recognition when you do reach out to them. Sounds a little stalkerish, right? In some ways it is, but it is all free public information. The stalker part depends on how you use the information, so be considerate when connecting online.

Networking online is very similar to in-person networking in many ways. Think about it. You need to show up with confidence and consistency. To be memorable, you must first be seen. Show up as an expert in your field by sharing relevant content, your own, and works from other people you can comment on and share.

> *Networking online is very similar to in-person networking in many ways.*

A photographer who works with young children will find most of their clients on Facebook and Instagram because these are great platforms to share their work and to connect with potential clients, parents of young children. So why spend a lot of time on LinkedIn and Twitter? On those sites, you want to have a presence with some activity, but your main focus should be where your clients are.

Have a daily and weekly plan for your social media. Pick a few groups on the platforms you choose and interact with them daily; comment, post, and share. Share great tips and information that will help set you apart as an expert in your field. The purpose of this daily and weekly activity is to create visibility, so people think of you when they or someone they know needs your services.

Pick A Place to Start and Do It Well

You don't have to be all places, be where your ideal clients and the people who know them are showing up.

> *Put yourself out there for your ideal clients to see you.*

The more they see you, the more opportunity they have to know, like, and trust you!

Be visible, be the expert. Share relevant and helpful content. Show up, serve others, get noticed, and get hired!

A word of caution... be covetous of your time, or you will get sucked into the vortex. Set a timer for thirty minutes maximum and schedule a time to interact on social media twice a day at most.

It's hard not to look when you are getting notifications all day long, I know! I actually turned off the notifications. I set a reminder on my phone to check once a day, this way I stay connected but don't spend all day there.

Select a Few Groups Relevant to Your Services and Your Ideal Clients

Think about your clients? What are they looking for? What kind of groups would be helpful for them? Think locally, regionally, and globally. Start with the name of your town and city and the word "network." Look at some of the groups where your clients are active members.

There's a lot more I could say, but I'm not the expert, and if you truly want to engage and grow your business online more than in-person, I recommend following a few social media experts who can help in this area.

Share Relevant Business-Related Content

Social media is a community, be a part of it by interacting and sharing regularly. Make a daily habit of posting relevant information others will benefit from. Follow other thought leaders in your field, comment on their posts, and share their content with your audience. It's really cool when you get a shout out from someone you admire for sharing and commenting on their content.

Content that connects is key, just like your thirty-second message. Tell a personal message or a story about something one of your clients has experienced that you were able to help them with. Be personable! Your readers want to get to know you and how you serve your clients. More important...people remember stories, tell them what they want to hear.

Just like your blog or newsletter, share what's important to your clients and repurpose content often. There are webinars and books on how to do this, and yes, it can be overwhelming. I suggest sticking with simple. Create a plan for sharing and stick with it.

For instance, I have a plan to post a new blog to my website on Thursday mornings, then it goes out in my newsletter on Thursday afternoon. It's scheduled to post to my social media platforms at least nine times throughout the week in various forms that always point back to my website or a download. When I follow the plan, my blog shows up in 9 locations over a week.

There are creative ways to repurpose your blog to attract more people to your website and help build your list. I suggest taking time to create a schedule or work with a social media expert to help you increase your consistency. There are several experts on the various platforms that offer simple tips and tools to implement a plan. My go-to person for training and action plans is https://facebook.com/SocialChicy/.

Use post planning tools that help you save time and block schedule content from going out. Again, some experts can help you with or do this for you. It doesn't have to control your life. Or you can just hire someone to do it for you.

Invite People to Connect and Like Your Page

Be sure to invite people to connect on social media. You can do this via your website, newsletter, business card, or a personal email. If someone connects with you or likes your page on Facebook, send them a personal message inviting them to connect on LinkedIn and follow you on Twitter and any other social pages you use for business.

A personal invitation goes a long way. People like to be invited! Ask their permission to send them your company newsletter. Just like in-person, ask to add people. Send them a message sharing the benefits of your newsletter and include a link for them to opt-in on your website.

Be Professional Online, Too!

Personal and Business Pages

Yes, you can have both a personal and a business page on some social media platforms. But remember, the people looking at your business page can also see what you are posting on your personal page because they are interested in learning about the true you before they buy.

Keep sales promotions and offers to your business page and share relevant content your ideal clients will be interested in on both. By content, I mean stories, blogs, videos, and images.

It is important to post regularly once you have a business page. Be sure to invite friends and business contacts to like your page and connect on your other social media platforms. If you spend a lot of time on LinkedIn, be sure to invite your followers from Facebook to connect with you there as well and vice versa.

Be Professional

Appropriate, relevant posting means just that, when posting, remember that you are a business professional and must act accordingly. Posting pictures of you drinking with friends may seem innocent, but not if you are trying to land a deal with a recovering alcoholic. Trust me, potential clients are looking at your posts.

You definitely need a little bit of personal mixed in with the professional, but you must be thoughtful and find a balance between the two. It is recommended that you keep your posts on personal pages to 80/20 split with 80% being personal and the rest being professional while your business page should be a 20/80 split. They are called personal and business pages for a reason. Most people on your personal page are friends and family who want to know what's happening at home, not work.

As you can see, professional spills over into personal and vice versa. Be mindful of what you post and where. Before posting anything, ask yourself...Is this something I want everyone to see? Is this something that would make someone uncomfortable or cause them to not want to work with me?

The best course of action is to share positive, inspiring information that will benefit others in some way, shape, or form. Keeping this in mind will help you avoid sharing inappropriately.

Please, whatever you do, please avoid foul language in print, video, and audio. It's offensive to many, so why take a chance of losing even one friend or follower over it.

Avoid Politics

Avoid politics unless you are a politician. Politics have a tendency to alienate potential clients. A lot of people avoid sharing their political beliefs, and they avoid people who share theirs. Most professionals prefer to keep politics out of the office, and whether we like to admit it or not, social media is an extension of your office.

Professional Bio

If you don't have a professional bio that you share on social media and aren't comfortable writing one of your own, hire someone to write it for you. Just like your website content, your bio is what potential clients are looking at. Make sure yours speaks to the specifics of how you serve your clients and why you are the best person for the job. It's not always about your credentials, often it's about your experience and your passion, so make sure your personality is reflected in your bio. A good writer will know how to help you find the balance. Think about what you look for in a bio. More important, think about what your ideal client is looking for.

Professional Headshots

Gone are the days of selfies and cropped family photographs, professional headshots are worth the investment. Again, you need to appear as a professional if you want to be taken seriously. That's not to say you can't have fun with it. If you are familiar with my images, you'll know that you can bring your brand into your photos. There are a lot of amazing photographers out there who specialize in creating branding with your images. If you are fun and funky, let it show in your pictures. No need for a suit if that's not how you show up for work every day, but be sure to invest in high-quality professional images you can use for social media, your website, and organization directories.

Remember...whether on-line or off, building relationships by serving others is the key to growing your business with the help of your network. When people know like and trust you, they share your content and help you connect with their network. Give them good stuff to share.

Make a Huge Impact

No matter where you network, online or off, these three actions will transform your networking outcomes:

✧ Follow up

✧ Show up!

✧ One-on-One Meeting

Have a system set up to help you with consistent follow up. I have a follow-up system and an email template for inviting people to connect that is simple and effective. Download it at **https://30secondsuccess. com/#get-it-now**.

Show up with consistency. Commit to going to every meeting and be there, and not just physically present but mentally present as well. If you know your schedule takes you away from home or keeps you in the office three out of four Tuesdays a month, then don't commit to a weekly Tuesday meeting, find a monthly meeting that works with your schedule or a different time of day that works.

> *Show up with consistency.*

> *One-on-One appointments are the lifeblood of networking.*

One-on-One appointments are the lifeblood of networking. This is where the magic happens. It's when you have the opportunity to sit face-to-face, one-on-one with people without the distraction of the other people in the room. One-on-ones are where great relationships begin to form. Be purposeful in inviting people to connect one-on-one.

Inviting people to meet with you "One-on-One" is simple once you have their attention. The best time to ask is during the networking portion of your meetings or afterward when you catch them on the way out.

Here are two examples of transitioning to a one-on-one meeting. When someone says something of interest:

I'd really like to hear more about XYZ; in fact, I'd like to learn more about what you do as well. Let's schedule a time to connect for coffee. Would in-person or virtual coffee work best for you?

After you've given them your response to "What do you do?", they will most likely come back with "How do you do that?"

I'd be happy to tell you more; in fact, I'd like to learn more about what you do as well. There are a lot of people here I'm sure we'd both like to connect with. Let's schedule a time to connect for coffee so we can learn more about how we may be able to support one another. Would in-person or virtual coffee work best for you?

Then pull your phone calendar out and book the date, time, and location! (Smartphones are great tools for connecting. Everyone has one, so use it to your advantage.) Be sure to get their card or contact info for your follow up and move on.

Power Partners

Identifying Your Power Partners

Power Partners are a crucial part of your business when it comes to marketing. This is especially true for entrepreneurs and small business owners who have a limited budget.

> *Power Partners are crucial to business success.*

As previously mentioned, meeting these partners and developing relationships that will help build your business is crucial to your success. I know this because these very people, these partners have helped me build my business from the beginning and still do so today.

Power Partners are business owners with similar or the same ideal clients. They serve the same people you do, network in similar circles, and have connections that will benefit your business. Likewise, you can do the same for them.

One of my clients, a bookkeeper, networks with a group of individuals who have similar clients. They work closely to understand how they support the same clients and how to help their clients and each other through referrals. She has even gone as far as adding her power partners to her marketing materials and website so clients have her list of trusted resources they can find quickly.

Learning who your Power Partners are and how to develop your relationships with them is the key to cultivating successful relationships.

Knowing how will help move your business forward faster through referrals, recommendations, and great business advice.

I first learned about the power of Power Partners from my LeTip group, a referral focused networking organization with local chapters worldwide. In this group, they encourage members to build relationships with Power Partners to grow their business and create more referral opportunities.

Referral networking groups are primarily industry exclusive for a reason. They encourage members to build relationships with Power Partners for the sole purpose of providing referrals for one another. Knowing how to offer good referrals is the key to these relationships.

To build these crucial relationships, you need to first identify who they are. You might be surprised by just how many people are your Power Partners. As you might recall from a previous chapter, I have at least twenty. Yes, I said twenty. When I began to focus on who my ideal clients are and who else in my network serves them, the list began to grow.

Here's my list of Power Partners for a Brand Communications Coach (Me!):

- ✧ Business Coach
- ✧ Brand Image Consultant Brand Photographer
- ✧ Videographer
- ✧ Social Media Consultant
- ✧ Marketing Consultant
- ✧ Graphic Designer
- ✧ Printer
- ✧ Promotional Product Rep.
- ✧ Networking Leader
- ✧ Career Coach
- ✧ Website Designer
- ✧ Banner Advertising Agency/ Advertising Agency
- ✧ Bookkeeper
- ✧ Accountant
- ✧ Business Attorney
- ✧ Trademark & Patent Attorney

110

- ✧ Corporate Event Organizer
- ✧ Corporate Trainer
- ✧ Expo Coordinator
- ✧ Business Advisor

Here is an example of just a few Power Partners I helped one of my realtor clients identify. Some may seem more obvious than others:

- ✧ Mortgage Broker
- ✧ Financial Advisor
- ✧ Title Agent
- ✧ Banker
- ✧ Home Organizer
- ✧ Home Stager
- ✧ Interior Designer
- ✧ Hair Stylist
- ✧ Manicurist
- ✧ Architect
- ✧ Home Inspector
- ✧ Contractor
- ✧ Painter
- ✧ Flooring Contractor
- ✧ Flooring Installer
- ✧ Exec. Placement Agency
- ✧ Insurance Agent
- ✧ Public Adjuster
- ✧ Accountant
- ✧ Bookkeeper

These people and many more serve the same clients as this Realtor. They are often privy to their clients preparing to move early in the process, often before a realtor has even been contacted. Understanding who your **ideal clients** are is the place to start. Identifying who else serves your clients is the next step to finding your Power Partners and developing relationships.

Finding Your Power Partners

Finding Power Partners really comes down to networking, building and nurturing relationships. Build relationships with your Power Partners by spending time with them at networking events and in one-on-one meetings. Invite them to other events where they will have an opportunity to network or meet some of your clients. This allows you to see them in action and experience the type of person they are and get to know them a little better.

Finding your Power Partners is all about who you know. If you're a natural networker, you probably already have several key people you rely on to help you with your business and refer your clients

> *Finding your Power Partners is all about who you know.*

for their services. If you aren't a natural networker, that is easy enough to fix with a little practice.

Identify who your key Power Partners are and keep them in a business card holder for quick reference or to share with people you are meeting for coffee. Show them the cardholder and ask if there is anyone they'd like to be introduced to. This will make for easy access and remind you to refer to them often.

Offering a complete package with your Power Partners as part of your team will position you as a valuable asset and as the "Go-To" resource. This can also open up more opportunities with larger clients for you and several of your partners. Collaborative opportunities begin to emerge when you team up with people you trust.

Remember my client who had a marketing brochure made and added her power partners to the back for all of her clients and potential clients to have at their fingertips? This is smart marketing! She made her company look bigger because of the resources she provides through her network.

> *Share your Power Partners with your network and clients.*

Regardless of how you go about it, share them. This is your team, your go-to people for help, the people you trust to send your clients to, and know that they will receive royal treatment because you sent them. Tell your Power Partners this, let them know what you expect, how you want them to treat your clients when you do refer them, and your commitment to do the same for their clients.

Evaluate your Power Partners from time to time. Check with the clients you have sent their way. Make sure that your clients are happy, this is the best outcome you can expect. You want everyone to benefit from this experience so that referrals continue to happen in all directions, through your clients and your Power Partners.

Educate Your Power Partners

Now, you might be wondering, "What do you mean, educate? Why do I need to educate them?" Well, perhaps like me, when I first started networking, your Power Partners may not be very familiar with this term or how to be a good Power Partner for you and your services.

It may take a little work on your part to identify your Power Partners and bring them together to help them understand that you can do a lot of good in helping grow one another's businesses. Yes, identifying who they are is the first step to building a strategic group of people who will support one another.

Here are some simple steps to building your own personal group of Power Partners (or Power Circle):

1. Make a list of what businesses serve the same clients as you.

2. Connect with these people through networking and asking other people for introductions.

3. Start to connect with these people regularly.

4. Get to know, like, and trust them. (If you don't...find new people.)

5. Spend time networking together.

6. Spend time connecting one on one and discuss supporting one another as Power Partners.

7. Ask the key question...What would you like me to tell people about you?

8. Educate them on how to refer you, help them by providing the right words.

9. Educate your clients, share your ideas on who they might need to work with next.

10. Listen for opportunities to refer your Power Partners to others in your network.

Copy this list and go find your Power Partners. Share this list with them and begin building your relationships and your business. Like all relationships, networking relationships take time to cultivate. Be patient and invest the time if you want the reward.

✏️ **Start your list of Power Partners by business, then fill in the names of the people you already have in your Power Circle.**

Support Your Power Partner

For many business owners and entrepreneurs, we sometimes feel isolated and alone, or we feel that we need fresh eyes to look at a project or idea. That's where Power Partners can make a huge impact on our lives, both professionally and personally.

When we take the time to build relationships with our Power Partners, we often find that it goes well beyond business. We start to care and to confide in one another. People are not meant to be alone; we need people we can trust to help us grow and look at the big picture stuff. We need them to help us dream and see a bigger vision.

Here are some ways to deepen your relationships, and, as you know, it all begins with trust. Earning the trust of your Power Partners is vital to building the strong supportive relationships you need to grow professionally and personally.

✧ Do what you say you will do. If you offered to make an intro-duction, do it. If you said you would call them to schedule a meeting, do it. If you said you would bring the donuts, do it.

✧ Send articles of interest. When you get to know what interests them, take the time to locate information that will be helpful to them both professionally as well as personally.

✧ Invite them to networking events or conferences you are planning to attend. Invite them to a sporting event, a party, or a picnic. Include them in celebrations with family and friends.

✧ Introduce them to the family. Invite them to dinner and include spouses or significant others. Sometimes the best way to get to know someone on a personal level is by spending time with them around their family.

✧ Hang out together. Find something that interests both of you and do it. If you both love the city, take a walk together. If you love golf, walk the course together.

✧ Spend time traveling together to networking events, you're both going anyway, so go together. The best conversations happen in the car...but remember, what happens in the car doesn't necessarily stay in the car. (That's an inside joke for my friends who ride with me and then see our pictures on social media later.)

✧ Talk "non-shop." Meet for coffee just to catch up and update one another on life outside the office.

✧ Look for opportunities to help them both personally and professionally. If they are moving, offer to help. If they are celebrating a graduation or wedding in their family, send a special care package to help get them through the day.

The point here is that Power Partners should be viewed as people who you will have in your life well beyond the point when you no longer own your business or have the same career, they become part of your family. Building trust by caring for them and taking that extra step to include them in your life is where it all begins.

Follow Up

Have you ever heard, "The fortune is in the follow up?" Well, they aren't wrong. Follow up is your opportunity to build credibility with your network. When you are purposeful in networking, you need to be purposeful in your follow up, or there is no purpose to any of it.

The point of networking is to meet people, to create interest, and to get them to want to know more. Now that you've done that, you need to take the next step, and that is building credibility and creating an opportunity to reconnect and begin building relationships.

Following up with your connections is critical after every networking event. Today I met a young man at the doctor's office. We had a brief conversation, exchanged business cards, and I told him I'd get him some information which I did as soon as I got back to my desk.

Part of building relationships within your network is your ability to follow up, your ability to build trust from the very beginning. When you meet people for the first time, it's about more than collecting business cards; it's what you do after the meeting that matters most.

> *It's what you do after the meeting that matters.*

Unquestionable Character

After your networking meetings or when you connect with someone during your daily outings, you need to follow up right away. Do what

> *Do what you say you will do.*

you say you will do. If you told someone you'd make an introduction, do it. If you said you'd add them to your email, visit their website, or call them to schedule a meeting, do it. When you do it right away, there's no opportunity to put it off or get distracted.

Many of my clients actually block 30–60 minutes out of their calendar after a networking event to make notes on business cards, send emails to follow up, and connect through social media. Then, they don't have to think about it later.

I know that life gets busy and busy people understand that, but being a person of good character matters in this day and age, and it shows people who you are, even when people aren't looking. This helps to build trust, and it's the first real opportunity you have to begin building relationships with your network.

One-on-One Meetings

The most natural step from networking to connecting is one-on-one meetings. This is where the magic happens. This is where you begin to build your relationships with the people in your network. Here's why one-on-one meetings work so well for building authentic, life-sustaining, intentional connections:

> *One-on-one meetings are where the magic happens.*

Know, Like, and Trust

This is where you begin to build that know like and trust factor that is a key element to people wanting to share you and what you do with their network. When you sit one-on-one with people, you have their undivided attention. This presents you with the opportunity to ask great questions and share more personal information with them than you would in a group. It gives you both the opportunity to get to know one another on a deeper level.

118

You also have the opportunity to help the other person understand what you do and how to refer you. As you know, two of my favorite questions when closing out a meeting are:

- ✦ Who would be a good referral for you?
- ✦ What would you like me to say about you and your business?

By asking these questions, you are essentially offering to help the other person grow their network through your connections. Be certain this is something you are willing and comfortable doing for this person. If not or not yet, ask for another meeting to become more comfortable with the person and gain a better understanding of who they are.

Inviting

Inviting people to meet one-on-one can be as simple as saying: "Let's schedule a coffee meeting. I'd like to learn more about what you do and perhaps discuss some opportunities to collaborate." (Note: Pull your calendar out right then and there and book it!)

You can also invite people via email. Be sure to remind them where you met and tell them why you'd like to meet. Here's an example: "Hi, Kathy, we recently met at the XYZ networking event. I'd like to continue our conversation over coffee. Perhaps we could meet in person, or if you are limited for time, we can make it a virtual coffee meeting via Zoom. Here's my calendar *(include a link to your online scheduler)* with both options. I am looking forward to connecting soon."

As I said before, virtual coffee is a great option for a lot of people. You get to see people face-to-face, spend time together, and save on travel time and expense. This allows for many more connections in a day, as well.

One-on-One Meetings

Get to know people! One-on-ones allow you to learn more about the people in your group, and it helps you connect on a deeper level and begin creating a bond of trust. Confirm your appointment via email or calendar invite.

> *Create a bond of trust with one-on-one meetings.*

One or two days before your meeting, reconfirm that you are still scheduled to meet and include the time and location. This helps to reduce last-minute cancellations and no-shows.

Prepare questions ahead of time. Ask questions about them.

- ❖ Ask what got them started, what they like about what they do, what their plans are for the future.

- ❖ Ask about their family, hobbies, where they live, where they're from, what kind of car they dream of having someday.

When you ask a lot of great questions, it breaks the ice, and they begin to relax and get comfortable with you. That's a feeling they'll remember long after the conversation is over.

> *Be unforgettable.*

Famous activist and poet Maya Angelou said, "I've learned that people will forget what you said, people will forget what you did, but people will never forget how you made them feel." Asking questions, expressing genuine interest in what they have to say, and taking the time to listen evokes a feeling of warmth people find hard to forget.

Make it about them! When they ask you questions, give a succinct answer, and then ask them another question. Eventually, the conversation will come around to you, but in the beginning, make it about them.

> *Make it all about them.*

Follow the "4-R" technique: Request, Response, Reply, Repeat.

Take notes on things you might want to remember to follow up on later. When they see you physically taking notes, they actively see that you are listening. This is one more way of creating that feeling of trust.

Respect their time. Be mindful of the clock and end promptly. If you find that you are fully engaged in conversation, mention the time and ask for permission to continue.

> *We build trust from meeting-to-meeting.*

As you wrap up your conversation, confirm what you will do for them (make an introduction, send them an article, invite them to another event, etc.) and then make the next appointment. We build relationships from meeting-to-meeting, never leave a meeting without setting the next appointment.

Be cautious not to fall into "Me too!" Listen to their stories and ask pointed questions that show you've been listening and express genuine interest in them. Remember...It's not about you, it's about them! Be intentional about the questions you ask and practice purposeful listening. You'll learn a lot about your network during one-on-ones, you may even learn things that surprise and delight you.

One-on-One Virtually

Busy people are starting to connect via virtual meetings. One-on-one in-person meetings aren't always convenient. Virtual is a great time saver.

Networking with people online allows for long-distance connections as well. You still see each other, spend time together, but save time on the commute.

Schedule a date and time for your virtual meeting. Schedule it using Google Hangouts or Zoom and send the link for the call in a confirmation email. Show up a few minutes before the designated time using your phone or computer. Be aware of your background, ambient noise, and appearance. Good quality image, sound, and connection make a good impression and reduce distractions as well.

Follow the "4-R" technique: Request, Response, Reply, Repeat.

✐ **Think about the people you want to connect with in your network and write their names down.** Make a list with notes of who they are, where you met, why you want to connect. This list will be a good memory jogger in the event you don't get to connect right away. Schedule time to call and invite them to a one-on-one meeting.

Here's a simple script to help you with the invitation:

Hi Stacey, I'd really like to get to know more about your business and how we may be able to support one another. Are you available for a coffee meeting? (expect a yes) Great, would in-person or virtual work best for you?

One-on-One Success

A successful one-on-one meeting is one in which both parties come away feeling good and feeling like they've been heard. Make them feel like they have a new friend. This can be accomplished by asking a lot of great questions about them and their business. Help them get comfortable by asking a lot of questions about them first, then move on to business. This will give you a better understanding of who they are and why they do what they do.

You can find some great conversation starters on the 30 Seconds Go! blog at https://30 SecondSuccess.com. *10 Conversation Starters* is a favorite **https://30secondsuccess.com/10-conversation-starters/** Questions should be more geared to breaking the ice before getting down to business. Enjoy your time together and don't be too serious, people want to know you.

Take notes! Be intentional about listening for their answers and take notes about them that will trigger referral ideas, follow up questions, and possible collaborations. Be sure to ask the questions mentioned earlier at the end of your meeting:

- ✧ Who would be a good referral for you?
- ✧ What would you like me to say about you and your business?

Next Appointment

If you like them and see more opportunities to work together and to build a referral partnership, set the next appointment. Continue building that know, like, and trust factor. Invite them to another meeting. Travel together to networking events, get to know one another by spending time together. Be genuine.

One-on-one meetings are all about getting to know the people in your network and growing together. Remember that networking at its core is all about serving others, your business will grow when you lead with a heart of service.

Follow Up System

Create a system for follow up that's easy and works well. Use your calendar to help you stay organized and on track. There are many apps and software programs out there that will help you manage your contacts. These tools are helpful as long as you use them and they aren't too cumbersome. Explore options and ask people in your network what software they use. I'm sure they will be more than happy to help; networkers usually are, and it's a great conversation opener.

Download the free "Your Follow Up System to Success," by visiting **https://30secondsuccess.com/#get-it-now**. This system includes simple strategies to implement and increase your success with follow up. It includes details about what to do with all the business cards you collect, sharing your calendar for easy appointment scheduling, and templates for inviting people to connect. It also includes a 31-day calendar that will help you connect and schedule the next appointment in-person or online.

Whatever your follow up process is, make it a habit by creating a system that works for you.

The Power of Referrals

The best compliment anyone can give your business is a good referral. When people begin to understand what you do and how you help your clients, referrals begin to come more natural.

> *The best compliment anyone can give your business is a good referral.*

A prime example is your doctor. If you love your doctor and you hear of someone who isn't happy with theirs, it's easy for you to tell them about your experience, and you'll most likely even provide contact info for them to find your doctor easily. That's what you want your network to do for you.

After years of tracking where my individual coaching clients have come from, it is no surprise to me that more than 75% of them have come from referrals. My network is where I started, and that has lead to the majority of my client work and many speaking engagements over the years.

Giving Referrals

Giving referrals doesn't come naturally to some people, though, we often need to teach our network how to refer us. The simplicity of showing by doing is sometimes the most effective. Develop your own system for providing good referrals for the people in your network and help them understand what a good referral looks like.

Here are a few simple steps you could set up and then share.

1. Ask them who they are interested in connecting with and write it down.

2. Check your contacts and see if there is anyone who might be a fit for them.

3. Call the person you want to introduce them to, tell them why you are calling, and ask if it is okay to make the introduction. This sets the expectations for both parties.

4. Send an email making an introduction that includes why you think they should connect and contact information for both.

5. Mark your calendar to follow up in a few days to ask if they have connected and how it went. This is a reflection on your reputation, so be sure to protect it by checking in.

Asking for Referrals

> *Be bold enough to ask for referrals.*

Sometimes we need to be bold enough to ask for a referral because people don't always see the same connections and opportunities we see. Asking for a referral and explaining why will help them better understand who you want to connect with, and perhaps they'll think of other introductions for you. Don't be upset if people agree to make the referral, but don't follow through as quickly as you'd like. Your priority isn't necessarily theirs.

To make it easier for people to refer you, send them a quick email blurb about yourself and why you want to connect. Ask them to edit and forward the message along with who you want it to go to. This makes life a lot easier, and it's a gentle reminder to them that they agreed to do this for you. Trust me, it works.

I know an amazing woman whom I am more than happy to connect with anyone in my network. She recently asked for some introductions, and I was happy to agree, only to forget once I got back to my desk and the distractions waiting there for me. She followed up with an email that included a brief intro asking that I forward it on her behalf to the three people in my network she wanted to meet. She made it easy for me to follow through, and I truly appreciate her for it.

Protect Your Reputation

It's your reputation, protect it. I say this with caution. Knowing the people in your network should ensure that referrals will go well, but you cannot always count on that. When making referrals, it is always helpful to let the people you are connecting know your relationship with the other person. Let them know if you have known each other for a while or if you are familiar but don't know much about their work. This puts it on the people you are connecting to do a little bit of research on their own.

> Protect your network and your reputation.

Follow the steps mentioned earlier for making introductions and mark your calendar to follow up a few days and weeks after the introduction. You want to ensure that it was a good introduction; after all, it's your reputation on the line. If it went well, great, be happy to refer them again.

If the connection doesn't go well and it can be rectified, do so. Sometimes people just have a bad experience, and it's a simple misunderstanding. Do what you can without getting in the middle of something major. Apologize if necessary, and move on.

If things don't go well and they can't be fixed, you might want to remove someone from your referral list. Your network is too important; your job is to protect them as much as you protect your reputation (and they know it). After all, that's part of the reason they know, like, and trust you.

Time to Evaluate

Evaluating your message and your network from time to time is imperative, especially if you've lived, worked, and played in the

> *Evaluate your message and your network regularly.*

same space for a long time. Sometimes clients come to me because they are bored with their messaging, or they feel like no one is listening to them anymore because everyone knows what they do.

I'd like to say this is the perfect time to evaluate your message and your network, but in reality, it might be too late. You need to keep things fresh and remain engaging. That's not to say you are boring, but some people just get bored easily. By changing up your message or changing up your network, you'll always have the opportunity to pique someone's interest.

Evaluate Your Message

Are you saying the same thing, the same way, to the same people every week for the past fifty-two weeks? Well, it's no wonder they aren't listening...they can probably repeat your message to you word for word without missing a beat. It's high time to change up your message.

Try touching on a different pain point for your clients or sharing something new you've added to your business. Share something they have not heard from you before or start your message with a question, raise your hand, and pause for effect to see who's paying attention and who isn't. (Hint: if no one raises their hand, it might be time to find a new group.)

One of the simplest ways to change your message is by telling stories. Have you ever heard the expression, "Words tell stories to sell?" Storytelling is one of the oldest forms of communication and marketing. It's the "pass it down the line" type of communication that has worked from the beginning of time. Yes, sometimes, the stories become larger than life as they get passed, but that might not be a bad thing when you want people to share how awesome you truly are.

Storytelling is a great way for people to connect with you on an emotional level, and stories are very memorable. By sharing stories, you give people something to recall

> *Stories are a great way to connect.*

when they connect with someone who might need your services. This opens up the opportunity for more referrals and business opportunities.

Remember to follow the formula (pain point, solution, call to action, & you) when crafting your message to ensure that you stay on point and on time. After all, we want to grab their attention and get them to want to know more so they can then tell others about you and how you help people by sharing your story.

Evaluate Your Network

I highly recommend evaluating your network every six to twelve months. Your business changes, as does your network. You might not necessarily need to leave a network to change it. If your network isn't working because of the people who attend, or the lack thereof, invite more people. Do your part in helping your network by constantly looking for and inviting people to join your group.

Bring quality individuals to your group that will help support every-one. Sharing your network with others is a great way to set yourself apart as a stellar individual, as a connector. When you go the extra mile to invite people to a great meeting you enjoy, you elevate yourself in their eyes and the eyes of the group. Again, it's about serving others. It's one of the things you can do to make networking a great experience for everyone. It's also a good way to set an example for others to follow.

Sadly though, sometimes it's hard, but we have to say goodbye. Sometimes we outgrow our networks to no fault of their own. Either they change or we do. Change is inevitable, but the question you need to ask periodically is...Is this still a good fit for me? By fit I mean, am I still able to contribute to the group; am I growing both professionally and personally because of my involvement here?

There is a saying that you are a reflection of the people you surround yourself with. Take a look around, do you like who you see? Do they have the qualities you want to reflect? Are they as willing to help you grow your business as you are for them? If so, great! If not, it's time to find a new network.

One word of caution, especially if the network is fairly new and you feel like they don't know the "right" way to network...don't give up on them too fast. They may just need some experience and a little bit of education on how networking should work. Hand holding and taking a leadership role may be the best way to build credibility and influence with a network in need of guidance.

My suggestion is to give them this book as a great tool to help them become better connectors. (Yes, that is a shameless plug, but, hey, we're friends now, so I thought I'd help you and your network become better connectors.) Seriously though, if it's a matter of people not knowing the proper way or the purpose of networking, maybe a little education is in order.

In Closing

Networking is about meeting people; true connection begins long after the meeting ends. How you attract people to you and your business starts with your thirty-second message and how you show up, but it goes way beyond that. It's about who you are and how you serve others.

If you think networking is about getting business after reading this book, you are sadly missing the point... it's about giving. The more you give, the more you make it about the people in the room and how you can enrich their lives, the more you will get out of it organically.

> *True connection happens long after the meeting ends.*

✧ Your thirty-second message is how you create curiosity and get your network to want to know more. It's the first step in your networking success.

✧ Networking, when done right and approached with a heart of service, can open many doors for you and your business. Changing your mindset to how you can help others is the second step in your networking success.

✧ Connecting is about relationships that serve you for a lifetime. Keeping the conversation going long after the meeting is over is the destination of your networking success.

Networking takes time and effort. If you don't like people, don't do it. Save yourself and the people who want to know you the time and trouble. If you like people, great! Commit to spending time with them, get to know them. They may not buy from you or refer you the 5th, 10th, 20th, or maybe not even the 50th time you've been together, but when the time is right, you position yourself as their go-to person. You do this by simply giving them the words to share with others when the opportunity presents itself, and that's where your thirty-second message comes in.

Thank you for reading this book. I hope you found it helpful and are already experiencing success with your thirty-second message. Share your thoughts and suggestions for future editions of 30 Second Success on the Facebook group page or leave a comment in the Facebook Group or email Laura@30SecondSuccess.com.

Wishing you much success,

Laura

Connect with @30SecondSuccess

Connect with @30SecondSuccess on Facebook, LinkedIn, YouTube, Twitter, Pinterest, & Instagram.

Join the Facebook group https://www.facebook.com/groups/30SecondConnect/

Sign up for the 30 Second Success bi-weekly newsletter. Visit https://30SecondSuccess.com today.

Acknowledgments

For God: Without you, these pages would be blank. Thank you for always being in my corner. You are my strength. All glory and honor to you.

For Elmer: Love of my life, thank you for believing in me and helping me believe in myself. You are my rock! I am so glad we get to dream and create what's next together. I love doing life by your side. LUMAMED!

For Elmer and Jessica: Thank you for your love, for believing in me, and for inspiring me to always try something new. Being your Mom has been an honor, a blessing, and the best job EVER. I love you both as big as the world! Never stop following your dreams.

For Dalton: Thank you for loving our girl, choosing to join our crazy clan, and for giving us the heavenly gift of grandchildren. Love you much.

For Clayton and Chloe: May you always follow your dreams and trust your hearts to lead you home. Never play life small and always know that G-Mom loves you as big as the world.

For Mom and Dad: Thank you, Mom, for your faith in me and teaching me to follow my heart. Daddy, you have shown me what it means to truly connect with people and to love this adventure called life, thank you.

For my Tribe: Thank you for listening to my crazy, for teaching me what sisterhood is, for lifting me up and dusting me off countless times, and for never letting me give up or go easy.

For my Amazing Network: Thank you for your support and encouragement, and for helping me find my way.

About Laura Templeton

Laura Templeton is the Founder and CEO of 30 Second Success, a company that helps entrepreneurs, professionals, and sales teams make better connections and obtain more business in thirty seconds or less. The foundation of 30 Second Success is built on crafting a brief message that connects with ideal clients on an emotional level. Laura is passionate about helping everyone find their personal message, thus giving them a voice to be heard. She lives in Bucks County, PA, with her husband, her son, and her office dog, Knox. Her daughter lives close by with her husband and two children.

Hire Laura for:

- **Public Speaker & Workshops:** For groups, associations, and organizations – offering tailored, interactive presentations focused on thirty-second messages and the value of networking and creating connections that audiences rave about. Think of me for your next event.

- **Individual Coaching:** A more personalized approach with direct feedback and guidance to develop 2–3 brand messages based on your specific networking needs. It begins with understanding your ideal client, where to find them, and how to create an emotional connection that ultimately increases sales and referrals.

✧ **Corporate Training:** Creating a company-wide message that connects is the first step to increasing sales. Training your sales team and your workforce to personalize and deliver that message is where the connection truly matters. Turn your entire company into your marketing team with the help of 30 Second Success.

Visit **https://30SecondSuccess.com/Services** to learn more and to schedule a call.

Sign up for our bi-weekly newsletter and schedule Laura for your next event or workshop.

Visit **https://30SecondSuccess.com** today.

Endnotes

1. Wilkinson College. "America's Top Fears 2018 – Chapman University Survey of American Fears." *Wilkinson College of Arts, Humanities, and Social Sciences*, 16 Oct. 2018, https://blogs.chapman.edu/wilkinson/2018/10/16/americas-top-fears-2018/.

2. Sinek, Simon. "How Great Leaders Inspire Action." *TED*, https://www.ted.com/talks/simon_sinek_how_great_leaders_inspire_action?language=en.

3. Farfan, Barbara. "What Is Apple's Mission Statement?" *The Balance Small Business*, The Balance Small Business, 5 Aug. 2019, https://www.thebalancesmb.com/apple-mission-statement-4068547.

4. "Fear of Public Speaking: How Can I Overcome It?" *Mayo Clinic*, Mayo Foundation for Medical Education and Research, 17 May 2017, https://www.mayoclinic.org/diseases-conditions/specific-phobias/expert-answers/fear-of-public-speaking/faq-20058416.

5. "380 High Emotion Words Guaranteed to Make You More Persuasive." *The Persuasion Revolution*, 21 Mar. 2018, https://www.thepersuasionrevolution.com/380-high-emotion-persuasive-words/.

6. McSpadden, Kevin. "Science: You Now Have a Shorter Attention Span Than a Goldfish." *Time*, Time, 14 May 2015, https://time.com/3858309/attention-spans-goldfish/.

7. "How Visual Attention Affects the Brain." *ScienceDaily*, 26 June 2013, https://www.sciencedaily.com/releases/2013/06/130626142930.htm.

8. Burg, Bob. *Endless Referrals: Network Your Everyday Contacts into Sales*. McGraw Hill, 2006.

CPSIA information can be obtained
at www.ICGtesting.com
Printed in the USA
BVHW030252071122
651319BV00017B/521

9 781734 376401